IN A CHURCH
DISMANTLED
ONE PILGRIM'S JOURNEY

*Finding My Way
Home in the Dark*

CONRAD L. KANAGY

IN A CHURCH DISMANTLED—
ONE PILGRIM'S JOURNEY
Finding My Way Home in the Dark
by Conrad L. Kanagy

Library of Congress Control Number: 2021952514
International Standard Book Number: 978-1-60126-779-5

Masthof Press
219 Mill Road | Morgantown, PA 19543-9516
www.Masthof.com

A Church Dismantled—A Kingdom Restored: Why Is God Taking Apart the Church? (Morgantown, PA: Masthof Press, 2021)

Ministry in a Church Dismantled: To Tear Down or Build Up? (Morgantown, PA: Masthof Press, 2021)

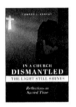

In a Church Dismantled the Light Still Shines: Reflections in Sacred Time (Morgantown, PA: Masthof Press, 2021)

Winds of the Spirit: A Profile of Anabaptist Churches in the Global South. with Richard Showalter and Tilahun Beyene (Harrisonburg, VA: Herald Press, 2012)

Road Signs for the Journey: A Profile for Mennonite Church USA (Harrisonburg, VA: Herald Press, 2007)

The Riddles of Human Society with Donald Kraybill (California: Pine Forge Press, 1999)

TO EZRA AND LEVI

You are loved, loved, loved!
You follow a long line of Unifiers and
Dismantlers, Disrupters and Dividers,
Priests and Prophets, all looking for a bet-
ter Home, a heavenly one.
May God give you the courage to journey
that same road to its glorious End!
Pappy and Grammy will meet you there!

"No aching for the future, gazing onward,
But calm resolve to honor even death."

—Reynolds Price, "A Whole New Life" (after Rilke)

TABLE OF CONTENTS

ACKNOWLEDGMENTS

This book, written over the past year, is the fourth in the series entitled "A Church Dismantled—A Kingdom Restored," based upon podcast episodes that I wrote during the Covid-19 pandemic. While the first three books are organized by themes, this one, which represents the most autobiographical of the four, is ordered—more or less—chronologically as the episodes came to me almost on a daily basis. Doing so allows the reader to observe my own journey from the beginning of the pandemic to the present. This process has been, as St. Paul describes the task of each of us, to "work out my own salvation with fear and trembling," dealing with the progressions of Parkinson's disease, teaching college courses remotely, and leading a conflicted congregation through the Covid-19 pandemic and the political polarization of this country.

To provide a contextual timeframe, each chapter indicates the month in which it was written. Most of these essays are previously unprinted material. The rush of nearly 280 episodes in eighteen months was a kind of pentecostal experience for me. You don't need to read the four books in any particular order. They stand alone but also overlap, each representing a different genre respectively: church growth and decline, leadership, devotional life, and memoir/autobiography.

I have so many persons to acknowledge and thank for their support of this project over the past year. I have walked this journey toward Home with my wife Heidi for longer and with far more depth and intimacy than anyone else—now for nearly 35 years. Neither of us can imagine completing the journey to its glorious End without the other.

Elizabethtown College for nearly three decades has given me space to engage in my church-related research and practice of ministry. Across four college administrations, I have been blessed by the same support and encouragement, without which I would not have been able to "pastor" as a minister and "profess" as a teacher at the same time. In keeping with what I have always experienced, the College has supported and promoted the podcast "A Church Dismantled—A Kingdom Restored" and has publicized my efforts widely. The College has also gave me a sabbatical for the fall of 2021 to continue writing and publishing my work.

Our congregation at Elizabethtown Mennonite Church has graciously been a space for me over the last decade to hone my preaching and writing for an audience that lives and labors in the everyday world of work, home, and play.

Dan Mast of Masthof Press has been a valued collaborator on this project and has postured himself to do whatever possible to speed this book along, to keep the pricing reasonable, and to add helpful counsel along the way. His staff has been amazing. Linda Boll has been sent by God to assist with the final editing and proofreading.

All but several of these essays were written during the Covid-19 pandemic. For the most part, I have sought to retain the present tense in which they were initially penned. This book and the podcast episodes that preceded it represent the intersection and integration of various areas of my professional and personal life that had been disparate entities in the past. They have allowed me to draw upon nearly three decades of teaching sociology, thirty-five years of sociological research, fifteen years of church and denominational consulting, twenty years of pastoral ministry, my childhood and coming-of-age in a conservative Mennonite-Amish community, my life-long struggle with a terror of God's wrath exacerbated by obsessive-compulsive disorder, and the diagnosis, four years ago, of Parkinson's disease.

As you will read throughout the chapters of this book, the Parkinson's diagnosis has been a challenging but transformative experience for me. Uncannily, it has represented my own dismantling while I have been writing about the dismantling of the church. But as you will hear me say repeatedly, this disease has given me a timeline and horizon that I had not seen so clearly before. It has brought with it an encounter of the love of God, a re-conversion to Jesus, and an outpouring of his Spirit in ways I had not previously experienced in my life, which has led to freedom, clarity of identity, and a sense of contentment like unto nothing I had known before. As I have often said, if it finally took Parkinson's disease to bring these gifts to me, then thanks be to God! For it may just be that these graces also ensure that I find my way Home through the dark.

So, accompanied by the gracious words of the apostle Paul, himself plagued by weakness and troubled with a thorn in the flesh that God would not remove, may you receive the words of this book, like St. Paul's, as means of encouragement. For, amid the dismantling: "We do not lose heart. Even though our outer nature is wasting away, our inner nature is being renewed day by day. For this slight momentary affliction is preparing us for an eternal weight of glory beyond all measure, because we look not at what can be seen but at what cannot be seen; for what can be seen is temporary, but what cannot be seen is eternal." (2 Cor 4:16-18 NRSV)

—Conrad L. Kanagy,
Elizabethtown, PA
November 30, 2021

INTRODUCTION
When My Story Unlocks Your Story

I recently received a note of appreciation for my podcast from an individual who also grew up in Big Valley, PA, but several years ahead of me. She began the letter by introducing herself in the way most of us do after years of distance and separation, explaining who we are by going back a generation or two and placing ourselves in the context that the other also shared and just might remember.

Older than I, I admired this person and her siblings for having left the Valley for parts I had never visited and for doing things I hoped to do someday. When our extended family would gather upon their visits to the valley, I always anticipated a conversation or question that might allow me to connect with them. So I needed no lengthy introduction in her email, for I remembered who she was immediately and had many memories of her and her family—this individual's quiet, kind and caring demeanor, the tragic passing of her mother, her father's critical comment in the pew behind me after I won the local VFW Scholarship, the birth of her triplet daughters, and more.

In any event, the writer shared that my podcast episodes had opened memories and stories of her own growing up in the valley, and then she offered what amounted to a prayer that is worth all of us praying these days: "I am being challenged to search deeper for armor to survive Covid-19 and the culture of my community, country and globe while hopefully being a beacon of love and hope. Some days are going better than others." There it is—both prayer and confession for what we need in this season of great anxiety and uncertainty.

Remembering our stories from the past is so important, for remembering reminds us that while we've not been in this particular place before, we've been somewhere like this place. And often that somewhere was when we were kids. We know that our earliest memories are usually those that most frighten us. I remember coming home at the age of two to find a car burning in our lawn, stolen and pushed down the hill to our house. I remember leaving that same house at Sylvanus Peachey's by the Kish Creek and again, just shy of three years of age, sneaking out of the house while mom washed the car as I was to be napping, and wandering up the through the Lutheran church cemetery. There the the caretaker found me and took me to Crissman's store nearby where someone was able to identify to whom I belonged. Remembering reminds us that we survived, and by God's grace will survive the rest of our journey Home.

Hearing each other and our stories give us the courage to go on in this broken and beat-up world. Hearing the stories of others gives us strength, hope, and faith to continue. When I responded to my acquaintance, I suggested that just as she had impacted my life in ways that I'm sure she was not aware of, so I'm confident that someone with her kind of heart continues to make a significant impact on those around her.

Because it is like moments within which we are living now, of anxiety and uncertainty and fear and doubt, even violence and oppression, that being a beacon of light has an amplified effect on the world. Kindness, grace, love, and compassion are heard so much more clearly in a context of division, anger, alienation, and darkness than they are at any other time. And because so many have given up even trying to shine their light, even the weakest efforts count for more than we know most days.

It is painful to see how Jesus has been highjacked these days by some who are doing the most violence in the world, causing the most pain to others, and picking on those who have the most to lose already. Sometimes I read to my students from the book of Matthew, chapters 5-7, when we are studying the theology of the Old Order Amish. I am intrigued by the fact that my students are largely unfamiliar with the Jesus of the Gospels. It's as if there are two or three different Jesus characters walking around in our world—the one of the Gospels, the one of conservative evangelicalism where Jesus joins the white supremacists and embraces a might makes right philosophy, and the one of the more progressive parts of the church where Jesus is stripped of his power to save and transform.

Why can't we just stick with the Jesus of the Gospels? I have half a hunch it is because Jesus usually told stories and listened to stories. He didn't develop a systematic theology, and he didn't waste a lot of time on ideas. Jesus certainly didn't talk about the headlines of the day—about the corruption of Herod and Caesar, the need to get out the vote to defeat Caesar in November, or how to solve the stock market's volatility. Instead, Christ used ordinary language and familiar stories as he talked about lost coins, lost sheep, a lost and rebellious son, lost gems, and goats that were rewarded instead of the sheep because the goats were so busy caring for the least of these.

The Pharisees rejected Jesus for a host of reasons, one of which I suspect was that Jesus' simple stories were the last things these scholars wanted to discuss; stories were for the children, for the unsophisticated, the non-professionals. And we reject Jesus too for similar reasons. Those of high status don't tell stories. They argue and boast. Those in power don't tell stories; they shoot people instead. Those in the top one percent don't waste time in stories, for stories won't earn another dollar at the end of the day. No, from the modern point of view, there just isn't much stock we can put in stories.

Except that when everything else is falling apart, and guns won't fix things, and when all the money goes down the tubes, and when politics implodes in on itself—all we are left with are our stories. But if all truth is God's truth, our stories are all we need, because for people made in God's image, inevitably we will start telling stories about the strange things happening in our souls and how we once felt close to God, and that dream we had as a child that we couldn't explain and on and on. Because though so often we have stopped listening, our loving Creator has never stopped speaking. It just might be that what my podcast listener was hearing was the voice of God echoing through the years with a message that I had quietly heard from her when I was a kid. Not only had I remembered who she was, but I had also remembered the qualities of grace that continued to be reflected in her letter.

The one thing that might hold us back from telling our stories and singing our songs is the fear that someone might challenge, reject, or deny our story. Some have challenged my stories. I expect to hear from others telling me that I got that date wrong, the number of children wrong, the location wrong, the year wrong, that my stories are no more important than theirs, asking what gives me the right to tell my story, or informing me that my story is offensive and on and on. But if telling my story unlocks your story, and your story mine, we just might both be saved from the hell breaking loose everywhere around us.

But who cares if our stories are rejected by others? If they were busy telling their own story, they would care less about what's wrong with mine. And at the end of the day, what is true about a story is more significant than the facts. For a collection of facts does not a story make. I've been a sociologist for more than 30 years; I've dealt in the arena of the empirical and social facts. But a collection of facts is not a story—not unless there is a heart smack in the middle of it.

So don't tell me what's factually wrong with my story until you can share your heart first, and then we can worry about the facts.

This is why I love the Bible still. It is true in the best and most authentic definition of the word. I could care less whether there are contradictions in the Gospels, whether early manuscripts disagree with each other, whether all archaeology supports the biblical record, or whether everything in the Old Testament lines up with everything in the New Testament. I've experienced that the Scriptures represent the only truth I need to meet the needs of my lonely and broken heart. What I know is that when I spend time in the scripture, I meet God. What I know in those moments is that I discover my story in God's story. And that story is enough for me now and forever.

Following my sermon one Sunday, which was focused on my grief over the losses that I and so many of us had suffered during this pandemic, I was approached by one of the saints who was concerned about what he had heard in my podcast. Taken by surprise, I hemmed and hawed from behind my mask. I was tired from having preached, especially since my message was filled with lament. I stuttered a few things about the podcast, trying to explain to him where I was coming from. And I'm sure I came across as a bit defensive.

As I turned away, the answer that I wish I had given him suddenly came to me from the titles to two old hymns I love: "Just as I Am, Without One Plea" and "Blessed Assurance . . . This Is My Story, This Is My Song." Accordingly, I thought, he may disagree with "my story and my song," and he may not appreciate me "just as I am." Nevertheless, "this is my story" and "this is my song." And I shall tell it and sing it forever in the presence of the One who receives me "just as I am."

There are so many reasons why I have hesitated over the years to tell my story and sing my song, but mainly because I feared the reaction of some of the saints. You know, don't you? Be careful, tread lightly, don't reveal yourself, I said to myself, as we all do. For we are bound like prisoners by specific social controls. Sociologists argue that family and friends' stigma, gossip, and rejection are the most potent controls we encounter. We have a hard time being our authentic selves, especially with those who supposedly love us the most. And yet, as sociologists also tell us, it is the stranger with whom we often are most willing to be transparent.

The fact is that the burden of self-shame is all too quickly conveyed to us from the moment we are born, after which the message we too often receive, hard-wired by negative reinforcement in the brain, is "I am of little or no worth." Sadly, this is the conclusion we come to about ourselves when most of all, we need to hear instead of the good news that God loves us and deems us to be of great worth despite all the falsities, pretenses, hypocrisies, and self-deceptions that plague our days.

As Evangelicals, we seem bent upon hearing, talking about, and critiquing others' beliefs. But seldom do we do a good job of listening to each other's life stories and validating one another as persons. Being fixated upon what we think others need to believe, we overlook what we most of all need for ourselves, which is an affirmation of our self-worth in the eyes of God and one another.

The same is true about the self-worth of others. We displace our unworthy sense of self upon others by holding them to standards of "right belief" that we are far from measuring up to. This is what Jesus pointed out when calling the scribes and Pharisees to task: "They devour widows' houses and for the sake of appearance say long prayers." (Luke 20:47a NRSV) Their unjust treatment of widows made hypocrisy of their prayers. Piety provided no cover for their injustice.

Unfortunately, "right beliefs" have become our public persona for many Evangelicals, the equivalent of long pharisaical prayers. We display our neatly bundled beliefs for others to see and adopt as their own. But what about our acts of justice and mercy? When we take an honest look at ourselves "just as we are," how do we measure up when it comes to our relationships with persons of color, LGBTQ+ persons, immigrant persons, and others? Do we treat them as any less worthy than we are of God's abundant acceptance and love? That is to say, if any such persons were to tell us their stories, speaking to us, "Hear me 'just as I am,'" would we open ourselves to them without prejudice and with the same welcoming compassion that Jesus bears toward each one of us?—"Just as I am, without one plea, but that thy blood was shed for me?"

At the beginning of the semester, I often tell my students to find a way to get "their voice out on the table," since together, we do not learn until we all have made our stories known. And that's because things will move from head to heart when we share our stories and songs with one another. When I have heard their hearts and stop worrying so much about what is in their heads, lo and behold, my own soul's longing to share my story and sing my song "just as I am" stirs within me.

In my sociology of religion course, I recently tried something different from my usual practice. I asked students to write their religious autobiography, even if it was about growing up without religion ("nones," meaning persons of no religion, is now an official religious category for us sociologists). I told them that the classroom is a safe place to tell their stories and to sing their songs and that we would not be critiquing or criticizing or judging one another's deep-down sharing. Their stories were to be grounded in their socialization, that is, in what they had learned, seen, and experienced at home, in school, in religious settings, and elsewhere. This was to be their time to reveal and explore together without being judged.

The results were terrific—honest, raw, moving, and deeply personal. As students listened to what sprang from the souls of others, the experience had a transformative effect on their beliefs. One person, who assumed that all Christians were right-wing supporters of Donald Trump, had previously declared himself an atheist. But having heard the stories of others, including Roman Catholics and Evangelicals who believed in God, by the end of the semester, he said, "For the first time, I now see that perhaps I can believe in God. I need some time to think more about this."

It wasn't his hearing about the beliefs of those Christians that opened his mind and heart, but rather it was hearing their deep-down personal stories. As a result, I walked away from the semester, grieving that the church provides few opportunities for honest conversations. We silence our need to express our beliefs long enough to listen to another's heart.

From toddler to grownup, Sunday school is frequently too much about believing the right things and talking about doing the right things, yet rarely about enabling our children and ourselves as adults to integrate the gospel from the biblical stories, including the stories of Jesus, with truth-telling about ourselves. For Jesus enters our stories not as a belief but as a person. Just as God does, Jesus cares and listens to who we are, to what's going on with us, to how we're doing, to what we're facing and struggling with, to our deepest longings, hopes, desires, and, yes, to our darkest moments of despair. "Just as I am, though tossed about with many a conflict, many a doubt, fightings and fears within, without, O Lamb of God, I come, I come."

When the church becomes a safe haven to tell our stories, we find more growth within our souls and ultimately much more love to offer one another. But when we are overly defended and protected by our beliefs, we miss the rich experiences of one another.

As with Truman Burbank in the movie "The Truman Show," the surrounding culture conditions us to live inauthentically within a walled reality, deprived of the fullness of authentic selfhood. Breaking away from those constraints, those walls do not come down quickly, for we must first disabuse ourselves of the "believed reality" that disguises the truth about our shared human condition. Truman believed from an early age that his father had been lost at sea, only to discover later with his very own eyes, and to his sudden shock, that his father lived as a homeless man on the street. We, too, require such moments of startling awakening. For it is then that we see what's transpiring not only within ourselves but also within others.

I wish I had broken through this kind of walled reality earlier in my life. I wish that doing so had not required the diagnosis of Parkinson's disease, which confronted me with the fact that my days were numbered and that if ever I wanted to become an honestly authentic human being, I'd better start now. I wish I had cared far less about what other saints and sinners (we're all a mix of both) had thought of me and about what I *believed* of what they thought of me. For I knew what no one else could possibly know about me until I shared it, which is the truth of my own deep-down story.

By God's grace and with thanksgiving, I finally broke through the wall. Yes, it's better to arrive home late than not at all. It's better to live authentically for a short time than to live inauthentically all of the time. Such breakthroughs, I believe, are God's way of preparing us to live in the richness and fullness of God's kingdom that, yes, begins now.

"Blessed assurance . . . This is my story, this is my song."

READERS' RESOURCES:
The website www.achurchdismantled.com contains resources to support the material in this book. Readers may subscribe at the website to receive weekly blog posts and series updates.

CHAPTER ONE

Got Jesus? Regardless of How
You Answer, Your Story Is Sacred
July 6, 2020

I've had the blessing of teaching at Elizabethtown College for nearly three decades, interacting year after year with the most delight-
ful students a professor could imagine. One of my favorite courses
is entitled Discovering Society, in which I introduce the basics of
sociology.

From the beginning of my teaching career, when I wasn't so
far from the students' ages myself, my goal was to speak to the basics
of being human. And why? Because if I couldn't convey at least that
much, then anything else I shared would hardly matter.

From my observations, I would regularly tell them that the
most successful people possess three qualities in common. They work
harder than others. They take risks no one else is willing to take. And
they "walk the talk," by which I mean that they live with integrity
and tell the truth. So I would say to them, "You can have the first
two qualities of hard work and risk-taking and yet still end up in the
police report or in the obituary section of the newspaper sooner than
you need to. But if you have the third and 'walk the talk,' then you're
going to do just fine because the world is dying for people like this."

From the very outset, I've also taught my students that their
lives are sacred. From my theological perspective, this means they were
created sacred and that, therefore, their flesh and bones are sacred, as
are their daily and lifetime journeys. This I believe with all of my heart.

1

Regardless of their religious commitments, lack of them, sexual orientations, experiences of trauma, criminal records, emotional and mental health challenges, or race or ethnicity, each is a sacred person.

To work with these most vital beliefs, I initially asked students to read Frederick Buechner's earliest memoir, *The Sacred Journey*.[1] Buechner spent his life as a teacher, ordained minister, and prolific writer. He is undoubtedly one of the most honest authors I've ever read, as is Anne Lamott.[2] Buechner's point is that God is always speaking to each of us and that our lives bear the mark of God's sacredness within us.

What do I mean by sacred? In human terms, the sacred is set apart as far more memorable than the everyday throw-away stuff of our lives. It's like the expensive dishes behind the glass window of the china closet or the occasions upon which we dress up in all our finery for grieving our sorrows and celebrating our joys, or the breaking of the bread and lifting of the cup at the Communion Table to eat and drink of the One who came and lived and died to say just how much we are loved.

The problem for us Christians is that we honestly forget that "God so loved the world" (John 3:16a), meaning that it literally is the world (the cosmos) that God loves. While we teach our children this familiar verse early in life, too often, we turn right around and live as if the verse reads, "God so loved the special people of the church." Without saying so, we imply that the rest of the world can go you know where! Our insider's language spells a tale of those poor souls outside of the church who just haven't gotten their stuff together yet, and we aren't sure they ever will. Yet, we will pray for them after we finish shaking our heads and talking about them.

---

[1]   Frederick Buechner, *The Sacred Journey* (San Francisco: Harper & Row, Publishers, 1982). See https://www.frederickbuechner.com/.

[2]   https://barclayagency.com/speakers/anne-lamott/.

The underlying issue then for us is that we may act as if a person's life becomes sacred only after choosing to love God, when in actuality "we love because he first loved us" (I John 4:19). The Psalmist sings of it.

> For it was you who formed my inner parts;
>> you knit me together in my mother's womb.
> I praise you, for I am fearfully and wonderfully made.
>> Wonderful are your works;
> that I know very well.
>> My frame was not hidden from you,
> when I was being made in secret,
>> intricately woven in the depths of the earth.
> Your eyes beheld my unformed substance.
> In your book were written
>> all the days that were formed for me,
>> when none of them as yet existed.
>
> (Ps 139:13-16 NRSV)

This is more than poetic truth, for it is the ultimate truth that pertains to each and every person that God has created. Every single one of us is a sacred creature of God's own making, with the sweetness of God's breath breathing life into us. This is true whether we have chosen to live our lives for God's good sake or not, which presumably is what some people mean simply by asking, "Have you got Jesus?"

I think that we who say we love Jesus would have infinitely more credibility if our love for Jesus revealed in us the ways by which Jesus universally loves. For then, we would begin to see that same love appearing within our families, friends, neighbors, and coworkers, regardless of whether or not they've "got" Jesus. Some of them might even dare to ask us about the hope that is within us.

Living and interacting with thousands of students across these decades has only increased my love and care for them as the sacred treasures they are in God's sight. I make it my task to encourage them in what is true and good, to call out the gifts God has placed within them, to share whatever wisdom I can from my own hard knocks, failures, and suffering, and to pass on to them my belief that their very being is of far more value than they may yet realize, especially when encountering frustration, doubt, discouragement, or untimely death, tragedy, or illness. For there is a sacred hope within them, whether conscious or unconscious, just as there is in all of us.

Having been diagnosed with Parkinson's disease has only strengthened the bonds that I feel with my students. Something about an old guy with a Ph.D., tremoring as he is in the classroom, creates a connection with eighteen- and twenty-year-olds who may not tremor on the outside but are quick to acknowledge they tremor on the inside. I'm not shy about sharing with them my faith and trust in the One in whom I have placed my hope, knowing I, like them, am of far greater worth than I have any idea—even on the days when I am tremoring the most inside or outside.

What I know is this. Every semester I have a classroom full of students who bear the distinct mark of God upon them, set apart and given a name uniquely their own, and loved with a sacred love that is from the foundation of the world, offered to them at the very moment of their birth. This means that I am called to love them just as Jesus loves them. And who knows? Maybe one or two or more of them will someday surprise themselves by saying, "I think I've 'got' Jesus." Or, more accurately, Jesus will have "gotten" hold of them in the sense of the prayer that he prayed to God: "I have made your name known to those whom you gave me from the world. They were yours, and you gave them to me, and they have kept your word" (John 17:6 NRSV).

CHAPTER TWO

Humpty Dumpty, the King and His Men, and "Dust in the Wind"

June 16, 2020

As a kid, like so many of us, I grew up hearing that familiar jingle: "Humpty Dumpty sat on a wall, Humpty Dumpty had a great fall, and all of the king's horses and all of the king's men, couldn't put Humpty Dumpty back together again!"

I have no idea where this little ditty came from or how it made its way into our little valley or how something so silly makes its way anywhere in the world, except for the fact that it harbors a central message that gets passed on from generation to generation. The message is this: "Don't fall, and if you do so, don't break. For there ain't nobody going to be able to put you back together again—not even the king and his men!"

And so we spend our childhood trying to balance on the edge of the wall, believing that if we fall, we are a goner and all is lost—that we will lie broken at the feet of the king and his men who will be powerless to put us back together again. This is a tough go for any of us—to chronically hang out on the edge of a precipice upon which one slight misstep could mean our doom. No wonder we all grow up so crazy with anxiety!

But what if falling was the antidote for our anxiety, and brokenness the beginning of our being put back together again? The one thing this ditty gets right is that it will never be the king and his men who put us back together because they are the last ones to recognize and appreciate the broken people, and the last ones to know what it means to identify with brokenness. They are too busy hanging on to the edge of their walls, which is tough to do while hanging onto a sword that if you fell, you might just fall upon.

But the research is pretty straightforward—that once we get to the point in our life where we recognize that we are broken and that there is no going back up on that wall, we begin to breathe a sigh of relief. We discover that we see the world differently from the bottom than from the top of the wall. We find others who have fallen from the wall and are also breathing more freely. We find out that we see the world more clearly from the margins than from the middle. And for once in our lives, we begin to understand that the king and his men are the ones to pity.

As a kid, I tried desperately to hold it together—to be good, act good, smell good, talk good, walk good—so much so that all those efforts created a chronic two-lane highway in my head. In one lane, I lived life—mowed the grass, prepared for exams, went out with friends, worked on homework, and on and on. In the other lane, I was preoccupied with maintaining "goodness," chronically asking God to forgive me for my failure to be so. My friends from high school remember seeing me pray quietly even as we played tennis, went bowling, and just hung out together (though they had no idea what I appeared to be saying to myself!). It takes a lot of work to drive in two lanes of traffic and avoid crashing into oneself.

By God's grace, I finally fell off the wall, and by God's grace, I keep falling off the wall. And every time I do so, something else that I thought was so good about who I am gets busted up because what I thought was so good about who I am is often simply what I thought others thought was good about who I am.

I will never forget reading, sometime during my college years, I guess, the Psalmist's words that God has compassion on us because God knows we are "but dust," that he knows that we have already fallen off the wall too many times to count and been trampled into broken pieces by the king and his men too many times to remember. And that God is just fine with that and prefers us that way after all. If we are comfortable enough with our brokenness to lie still and wait, somehow through it all, God begins to put us back together—not the way others think we should be but the way God who created us knows we were made to be.

The shame is not in falling off the wall. The shame is not in being so broken that only God can put us back together. The shame is that the church fails to have compassion for those most broken and assumes that ultimately it will be the king and his men who put us back together again. No thanks—like Kansas sang when I was a college student just beginning to listen to pop music, we are all just "dust in the wind," being blown along wherever and whenever the Spirit wills. And the freedom of the breeze and the scenery it stirs up sure beats clinging to the edge of a wall and the view of the king and his men.

CHAPTER THREE

Fallen Tree, Chihuly Blown Glass, and a Dear Friend to Help Me Get Home
June 19, 2020

On February 14, 2017, I heard those exact words again at the University of Penn Medical Center regarding the Parkinson's tremors I had experienced.

"I don't think there is an alternative diagnosis"—which was no more than a reiteration of what I'd heard from my family physician when he said, *"Boy, you sure don't want to have this disease—it's all-encompassing."*

Neither statement offered much hope. I quickly discovered that viewing my situation from the standpoint of medical science offered me little to no *ultimate* hope.

Before I learned of my diagnosis, by God's grace the congregation granted me a three-month sabbatical, which we were to embark upon later that summer. It was a providential gift. It allowed Heidi and me time to process together the excruciatingly painful and discouraging news we had received. It also spared us of the glare of earnest questioners until we first had a chance to listen deeply to God. And, as is so often the case, God's words for us came from a variety of unexpected sources.

The first was from a visit to the Chihuly Garden and Glass exhibit in Seattle, Washington. If you've ever seen the work of artist Dale Chihuly, then you'll understand why any attempt of mine to describe it can't begin to express the grand mystery and beauty of it all. What intrigued me most was that part of the exhibit that described Chihuly's change of artistic expression due to the onset of his disability.

"After losing sight in his left eye and dislocating his shoulder," the description stated, "Chihuly relinquished the gaffer (the 'boss') position and began drawing as a way to communicate his vision and designs to his team. The drawings evolved beyond a communication tool to become an important part of his expression." Chihuly later concluded, "Drawing really helps me to think about things. I am able to draw and work with a lot of color, and that inspires me."

Here was the first hint that my own dark, all-encompassing life-sentence to Parkinson's disease could be an opening to new creativity and joy, to a new way of revealing to others what lay dormant within me.

It was by his giving up of the "gaffer" position that Chihuly's students were empowered to do what he had done so well. For it was by picking up his brush that Chihuly revealed to others the vision he saw for himself. Up to that point, all that anyone could see of the artist was the grandeur and beauty of his art. But now, enabled by an awareness of Chihuly's disability, they could see into the heart and soul of the man, from whom the grandeur and beauty emerged. Dale Chihuly's disability had provided the giant leap into his maturation as an artist and a mentor. It is no surprise, then, that his drawings now sell for thousands of dollars.

The second window of divine opening to my "Parkinson's self" came during our trip to the Olympic National Forest, which displayed a mystic beauty eliciting considerable awe.

As we hiked the trail, taking photos of gigantic trees standing in majestic splendor as they had for centuries, there appeared a lone tree that I would not have noticed, except for the fact that it had fallen partway across the trail but remained about eight feet above the path. Despite its misfortune, it had bent itself upward toward the infinite sky. It was that tree, among the other grand, straight, and upright ones surrounding, that caught my eye. I beheld it, not for its perfection but for its persistence—living, breathing, and rising in its crooked, twisted form—persevering against daunting odds, revealing an unparalleled beauty all its own.

It happened just then. As I stood before that arched inhabitant of the forest, I sensed myself more present to my life than I had ever been before. Perhaps, I thought, my own disability would now render me more useful than I could possibly imagine. Who knows? By God's mysterious providence that hobbled tree may have been positioned this way for decades. And perhaps for the singular purpose that all passers-by, lame or laden with burdens, might trace its visage aloft, drawing light and strength from heaven above.

Finally, yet another divine opening during our trip, appeared in a passage from a book about Sabbath rest. It helped me realize that the disease of Parkinson's would make me considerably dependent upon others, more so than I was ever willing to be in the past. I began to see that the gift of dependency could be one of the greatest gifts I could receive or offer in return. For God didn't create us to live independently of one another, nor independently of God himself. Why is it, then, that we think we can go it alone as if we must prove to ourselves, yet certainly not to God, that somehow our independence makes us invulnerable and invincible?

Wayne Cordeiro, in *Leading on Empty*, notes this truth: "When we wrestle with our own infirmities, we are not disqualified from God's plan for our lives. It may just mean we will arrive at it differently from the way we had intended. We may arrive leaning on the arm of a friend."[3]

---

[3] Wayne Cordeiro, *Leading on Empty* (Bloomington, MN: Bethany House Publishers, 2009), electronic edition, 155.

For me, that thought hurled light into my darkness, causing me to view Heidi, my dear wife, in a way I had not seen her before. With my Parkinson's disease, I would need Heidi more than anyone else in order to find my way home. And that recognition alone deepened my love and thanksgiving for the extraordinary gift that she is to me.

I needn't pretend anymore that I could go it alone. The mask of my independence had fallen away. The façade of my self-sufficiency had fissured and snapped like a dead limb breaking away from an aging tree. I had come to experience what Paul, that Jewish-Christian mystic and ambassador to the Gentiles, so eloquently wrote to the church at Corinth. It is worth our hearing Paul repeat it.

But we have this treasure in clay jars, so that it may be made clear that this extraordinary power belongs to God and does not come from us. We are afflicted in every way, but not crushed; perplexed, but not driven to despair; persecuted, but not forsaken; struck down, but not destroyed; always carrying in the body the death of Jesus, so that the life of Jesus may also be made visible in our bodies. (2 Cor 4:7-10)

Somehow, by the mystery of God revealed in Jesus Christ our Lord, the depth of our inner darkness disperses when encountering the brilliance of his light, even as the unveiling of our weakness reveals the abundance of his strength.

As Paul professed, "This slight momentary affliction is preparing us for an eternal weight of glory beyond measure." (v. 17)

So, if by chance I'm ever that Parkinson's man you see hobbling along the sidewalk, crouched over with age, with creases in my face, with shuffling feet, with cane in hand and a limp in my gait, then may you remember to see me just as I saw that fallen tree—bent over, to be sure—but turned upward, yes, yes—by the Light.

CHAPTER FOUR

Mennonite Central Committee, a New Doctor, His Young Family, and a Trip to the Philippines

July 1, 2020

Very truly, I tell you, unless a grain of wheat falls into the earth and dies, it remains just a single grain; but if it dies, it bears much fruit. (John 12:24 NIV)

...but he said to me, "My grace is sufficient for you, for my power is made perfect in weakness." So, I will boast all the more gladly of my weaknesses so that the power of Christ may dwell in me. Therefore I am content with weaknesses, insults, hardships, persecutions, and calamities for the sake of Christ; for whenever I am weak, then I am strong. (2 Corinthians 12:9-10 NIV)

And not only that, but we also boast in our sufferings, knowing that suffering produces endurance, and endurance produces character, and character produces hope...(Romans 5:3-4 NIV)

One of the most rewarding courses I teach includes a project where students write the story, from a sociological perspective, of someone in their family tree who was born before 1950 and then present that story to the class at the end of the semester. The students love this project, and there have been many exciting outcomes—one student asked an attorney to read the will of her grandmother, and in doing so, discovered that their grandmother had actually willed the family homestead to the student's family. The family had been told that the grandmother had willed the home to her second husband, who had taken ownership of it.

Another student's grandfather, as he was writing about him, suddenly died during the semester. Another interviewed an individual about his life, only to learn that he died the following day and that she was the last to have ever discussed his life with him, and another's mother passed away suddenly and the student asked if she could process this loss through her paper. One of the qualities that the students consistently identify in the stories they tell is the suffering and challenges that those born before 1950 experienced and how resilient they were in overcoming and persevering, and finding ways to become stronger through suffering. They also consistently identify the strength of the communities where these individuals lived compared to what they as students experience now, particularly terms of in religious and family communities. I have encouraged my students not to run from pain and suffering but to recognize the strength they have to persevere and that suffering will, throughout their lives, be their most excellent teacher. And I have quoted St. Paul's words about suffering leading to perseverance and perseverance to character and character to hope.

Three years ago, the Mifflin County Mennonite Historical Society celebrated and remembered the life of my wife Heidi's grandfather, Jacob James Brenneman, a man whom Heidi always called Poppy and whom she dearly loved. As Heidi prepared to share that evening, she discovered documents related to her grandfather's decision to go with Mennonite Central Committee (MCC) to the Philippines in 1946 to help develop and offer much-needed medical care following WW II. In his reflections, Poppy or Dr. Brenneman says this:

Upon my return to my home in Hesston, Kansas, Mrs. Brenneman and myself talked and prayed over the matter, and we were led to the conclusion that I would go if the way opened for me to leave for a year and one-half of service in foreign relief. The way seemed to open and on May 28, 1946, we finally decided to dispose of my office, equipment and medicines and engage in the field of medical relief in the Philippines for a term of one and a half years. Naturally enough the disposing of one's office, his equipment, his office supplies and medicines was no easy task. When I gave the key to my successor and walked out of my office door for the last time my heart was heavy within me and my eyes did show some moisture. I had been in the office almost four years and was naturally quite attached to it.

In another document, Dr. Brenneman described the last moments with his family before departing:

The final parting came at 7:30 p.m. of July 31, 1946 on the platform of the Pennsylvania Railroad station in Lewistown, PA. We were quite well prepared for the occasion, but to say goodbye and part for a period of 18 months is no easy task especially from one's dear wife and sweet little babies. I gave little Gwendolyn her goodbye kiss at home because she did not accompany us to the station...I gave each one in turn a goodbye squeeze and kiss and finally came to my dear Maude and it was almost too much. Yes, and eyes were wet and our hearts were heavy, but were sure we were doing God's will. The train pulled up and my things were put on and "all aboard" echoed out and I was off by myself. The picture behind was deeply impressed in my mind and I shall never forget it...Maude had tears in her eyes, but just as the train pulled out and I waved goodbye a beautiful smile broke through the tears and our parting was complete.

In a season when many of us are anxious about the uncertainty of our lives as the result of the Covid-19 pandemic, Jim and Maude's shared decision to step from the security of private practice as a physician into the uncertainty of leaving family and community to serve the poor and oppressed is a reality check for us who so much want to avoid suffering rather than embrace it, who want things to return to normal rather than being willing to accept the growth opportunity that comes with the abnormal. The Brennemans' story reminds us that saints do not so much seek comfort as give it up; settle down as much as to keep on moving wherever God leads.

The opportunities for sainthood are all around us these days—the injustices facing black and brown folks, the poverty and homelessness in our local communities, the children and single parents right around the corner from us, those who have lost their jobs—and on and on. I wonder how much of our concern about getting back to normal for American Christians lies in our desire to return to the kind of comfort, security, and familiarity that Dr. Brenneman relinquished to Jesus when he boarded the train in Lewistown and said goodbye.

Dr. Brenneman would return from the Philippines, and he and Maude would set up a medical practice in their home in Belleville. And eventually, they would have a granddaughter named Heidi, who hung out much of the time in Poppy's office and in Poppy and Granny's home. And Dr. Brenneman would treat my family and hundreds of other families over the next several decades until he passed suddenly of a heart attack at age 69 in 1980. It has not been unusual for Heidi to meet people who gratefully, and some in tears, describe her grandfather's care for them or someone else at some crisis point in their lives, including hundreds of folks whose children were delivered by Dr. Brenneman in their home. While coming across a bit gruff to others sometimes, there was also something saintly about Dr.

Brenneman and Maude—something undoubtedly that emerged in the crucible of those years apart.

Oh, how we wish for another way, for another equation that might begin with perseverance and produce character and hope without the suffering. Of course, the truth that suffering is the pathway to sainthood flies in the face of a culture that research shows to be increasingly narcissistic, that prefers to demean and bully and objectify the other rather than recognize our shared humanity and suffering. But Jesus makes it pretty clear that any chance of developing virtues worth remembering and taking to our grave always begins with our own experiences of loss and suffering and even death. For nothing teaches us our shared humanity, like suffering. And nothing creates true community like suffering. And as many of us have learned, nothing produces hope like suffering.

I am grateful that I do not have a theology that teaches me that in this life, bodies should not be broken, that the world should not be broken, that the church should not be broken, or that the brokenness of any of these somehow means God is impotent and that we are without hope. But instead, it is in these realities of life, where we find our only hope.

I do not doubt that among you who have already given up so much and have observed and experienced so much suffering, none of this is news to you and that you could probably tell it much better than I. Still, I trust, nonetheless, there has been within my thoughts something that encourages you to continue traveling the path of our suffering Lord until that day when all of creation will sing a new song.

Indeed the broken will be whole, the sick will be healed, the traumatized will be safe, those in exile will be home, and together we will join around the throne of the One who took up our sins, carried our sorrows, knew our most significant suffering and was in it with us, was wounded so we might be healed, and whose punishment brought us peace, shalom and wholeness. And it is in looking back that we will be able to see that in some small ways, not only did our suffering reflect his, but the hope we brought to the world did so as well. But I do wonder what has changed for us over the last 70 years such that our primary question in this pandemic is how do we get back to normal and to church rather than how do we leave what is normal and also leave church behind for the sake of the world that God so loved and so loves still?

CHAPTER FIVE

Why I Am Still an Evangelical and Mennonite—Wheaton College, the Leverage of Love, and the Anabaptist Churches of the Global South

July 5, 2020

I've received a question from at least one listener that went something like this: "You are identifying with Evangelicalism in your writing. Why? I no longer do because of the identification of Evangelicals with the political right."

This question gave me pause since I have been very intentional in specifying my evangelical identity and commitments as I write. I do so because my faith as a young adult was most formed by my experience of Evangelicalism at Wheaton College in the mid-1980s. I was a kid who grew up between two mountains where there were few influences other than the deep cultural and spiritual and rich heritage of Amish and relatively conservative Mennonites. There was little room for nuance or ambiguity. The clean lines of the mountains created clean lines theologically and sociologically.

When I went to Wheaton College, I was a kid looking for a faith home even if I didn't know it. I was also a kid who was tormented, growing up with my fear of hell's fires, my unworthiness before God, my inability to find peace with God, a clinical case of obsessive-compulsive disorder that was religiously focused, and one for whom my mother's prayers in the middle of the torment likely saved my salvation if not my life.

But getting to the Midwest, the mountains were gone. Chicago was big and inviting. My friends came from all over the country and world and believed differently than I did. In a course in my freshman year, I was introduced to Martin Luther's *Freedom of a Christian*, and for the first time in my life, I had hope that there was a God who was not waiting to pounce on me the moment I broke his rules.

Even though in that same class I failed my first college exam—because I had missed the part where the professor said we would need to memorize "A Mighty Fortress Is Our God," and thus assumed I had also failed out of college within the first four weeks—that course had a profound effect on me. It offered me a ray of grace that I had never seen before. It provided me a glimpse of a loving God I had never known before. And while it would be decades before that hope and love expanded to overcome the religious torment in my head—the introduction to Luther alone may have kept me in the faith.

And there were so many other rich experiences at Wheaton College. Chapel services with the best of the best in terms of spiritual depth. My friends were all on a spiritual journey to figure out who God was and whether indeed he even was—Bill Motz, Bob Baker, Rod Buikema, Steve Weiss, Mark Ritchie—and many others. I found freedom in these relationships and in the context of an evangelical college where the faculty were fully engaged in learning and who excelled at their craft. Phrases like "all truth is God's truth" and the "integration of faith and learning" have never left me. The influence of Dr. Arthur Holmes on campus, the open-mindedness of President Richard Chase, the deep concern for social justice of Dr. Wayne Bragg and the HNGR program, all influenced my understanding that to love Jesus meant to love learning and to love the truth regardless of its origin.

I spent six months in Ecuador doing a sanitation development project and research on the Quichua peasant's mass conversion to Protestantism in the 1960s, resulting in my first professional publication under the supportive mentorship of Dr. Jim Mathisen. Dr. Mathisen had a lot more confidence in me than I had ever had in myself.

It was at Wheaton College, walking across campus by the "BSC," tortured by what to believe or whether to believe anything about God, that I stopped and said, "I choose to believe that God exists, I choose to believe that Christ is God and came to earth to reconcile me to God, and I choose to believe that the Bible is real and true." That's it. If I don't believe something soon, it will drive me to the edge of sanity's cliff. And so, at that moment, I chose to believe and have not looked back since. As C. S. Lewis suggests, upon arriving at the choice of faith, one begins to see what one didn't see before that choice. And that was true for me as well.

It was a choice for me to be an Evangelical, and a choice that no right-wing conservative Christian who has tied their soul to politics will ever take away from me. Why would I give them that power? What the evangelical right-wing has co-opted from classic Evangelicalism is not Christ—it is essentially a mirage that in appearance is close enough to look convincing to many—far too many. I don't know what folks will do when their political allegiances don't come through for them—turn back to Christ, I hope. If not, this movement will eventually lose its commitment to Christ because the appeal of this world's power is too great.

But I am also a Mennonite, and that story is shorter than the last one. It came down to love. I was dating and engaged to be married to Heidi. She had grown up at Maple Grove Mennonite Church. She found her own spiritual home—safety, security, friendship, leadership in Allegheny Mennonite Conference, and love for Jesus that transformed her. She was not leaving her home either.

And so one evening as we were driving—and I remember exactly where we were on Route 322 between Reedsville and Burnham, PA, I looked at Heidi and said that I might not always be a Mennonite. She looked back and said something like, "Well, then we won't be getting married." And that was the end of that story. I am so glad that not only did I marry Heidi but that she kept me in a spiritual home that I have come to appreciate more and more the older I get, even though it too has been co-opted by a host of societal influences. But again—regardless of what that label means to others—it too is my home, and I am grateful for it and will continue to claim it as the one that is closest in my mind to "what Jesus would do."

In 2007 I published a book entitled *Road Signs for the Journey*, in which I described a study of the Mennonite Church USA that I had conducted in 2006-07. I used the book of Jeremiah as a kind of foil around which to wrap the story of our denomination, a story that left me and many others deeply demoralized: rapid aging, increased political engagement, ongoing racism, loss of commitment to scripture, evangelism, and a decline of the peace witness and more. It was a moment of soul searching for me about the church in general but my Mennonite commitments in particular.

But shortly after that, I would conduct two studies of the global southern Anabaptist churches. The experiences of faith, the awareness of the Spirit's presence, the commitment to social justice and reconciliation, and the growth of local congregations that I found among these brothers and sisters in Asia, Africa, and Latin America were like an oasis in the desert where I had been dwelling, and gave me renewed hope that Anabaptist and Mennonite expressions of faith might remain vital long into the future.

And so I am and will remain Evangelical in the truest sense of the word and Anabaptist in its most faithful expression of the Gospel of our Lord!

CHAPTER SIX

The Imperials, "We Built This City on Rock and Roll," and Running From Sodom and Gomorrah (or from Goldie Hawn and Burt Reynolds)

July 14, 2020

I keep hearing the song in my head, "We built this city on rock and roll," by Jefferson Starship. It's crazy, really—I never remember it as a favorite of mine, nor do I have any idea how it popped into my mind a week or so ago. It's considered a terrible song, voted several times as the most hated pop song in America. I don't know why it is hated so much, but then I'm no judge of rock and roll since I grew up in a home where rock and roll was strictly prohibited. Any hit songs from the 1960s and 1970s are entirely missing from my pop culture repertoire unless I've picked them up since by virtue of others who were tuned in during those decades. It's pretty clear to me that missing 1970s pop music wasn't missing much, but the 60s are, of course, a different story and one I've managed to recover in part by marrying someone who grew up with those hits echoing through her home.

But sometime in the early 1980s, I stumbled into contemporary Christian music, perhaps by one or two tunes that inadvertently showed up on WDAC. This Christian radio station also brought us a host of kid's radio shows like Ranger Bill and many others. One day I brought home my first album. It was by the contemporary Christian group, the Imperials, and I bought the album with hard-earned cash. I was proud of my new purchase and wanted everyone in our family to have a listen. I think the only song of the Imperials I probably knew was "Sail On," which hardly rated as rock and roll at the time or any time for that matter. It certainly, however, did have that smooth, synthetic, polyester feel to it of the late 1970s.

I opened the lid of our five-foot-long stereo cabinet and plopped down the vinyl, placed the needle, and off we went. I should have begun with "Sail On" because little did I know that the lead song on the album sounded like some sorry version of perhaps AC/DC or the Rolling Stones. Seeing Dad's reaction, I quickly recognized that any future listening to my new purchase was up for grabs, and so I panicked—"But Dad!!" The song began as a kind of cross between screeching and wailing and lyrics of "I'm going down to the river, my Lord..." and that was about as far as we got because Dad had already heard enough. "There is not going to be any rock and roll in this house," and I suspect added the familiar strain of, "If you want to do that in your own house someday, that's fine, but not as long as you are under our roof!"

It was a big enough deal that my brothers clearly remember the episode as well. Perhaps because it was one of the few times I, as the oldest brother, managed to pave the way for more significant opportunities for their deviance down the road—I was the ultimate conformist. Because compared to what else was being played in the 1980s, the Imperials would end up sounding like monks at morning vespers.

Looking back, I am now, for the most part, glad that my parents had a skeptical eye toward modernity and pop culture. It meant I spent my days with my brothers by the creek or stalking squirrels with my 20-gauge shotgun after school, hiking in the woods, reading, fighting with my brothers, and a host of other activities that probably saved my brain cells and opened up a world of creativity for me.

Sociologist Max Weber had quite a skeptical attitude toward modernity more than 100 years ago, as did the German critical theories of the 1950s, who added to his skepticism a criticism of celebrity and entertainment culture as well as the commodification of just about everything. Unfortunately, as Evangelicals, our eyes have often been less discerning of the culture around us. The more we've moved into the center of that culture, the less wise we've become. It's why I am glad I grew up on the margins of pop culture. Because it's on the margins where we are most likely to be able to see what's wrong with the center—wrongs that can't be observed otherwise.

My first theater experience was as a freshman at Wheaton College, where a group of friends and I went downtown to see Rocky II. We didn't have television at our house, nor were we permitted to go to the movies. I still remember walking into the dark of that theater and the discomfort of being in a place, that by the time I was 18, my brain was hardwired to see wickedness and evil in every corner. But I settled in and watched Rocky overcome the odds once again, and I didn't sense any evil spirits around after all.

My friends convinced me to try the movies again sometime later, and since I had survived the first time, I agreed. I didn't know what we were watching or who the actors were, of course, nor do I remember the plot if there was one. But I do recall the horror of suddenly seeing Goldie Hawn and Burt Reynolds getting it on in a way that I knew was precisely the reason I had been forbidden from going to the theater in the first place as a kid.

I panicked—not knowing whether to close my eyes or slide down in my seat. Instead, I chose to run. I muttered to my friends, "I got to get out of here!" I think they probably wondered what was wrong with me since that action on the screen was probably what brought them there in the first place. But I was having none of it, and out through the dark row and center aisle I went, running from that den of iniquity as fast I could. Looking back, I don't know if I thought it was the devil or God breathing down my neck. Sadly, it was also true that I didn't distinguish very well between the two in those days. My friends later returned that evening, and I don't think I ever told them what made me leave just as the good part was beginning.

But back to Jefferson Starship, and "We built this city on rock and roll." It turns out that there was a lot of tension within the band as it evolved through multiple stages over the years, and the tension was in part about what it meant to be modern and what modern music was really meant to be. Given the hatred folks had for "We built this city on rock and roll," the group must have failed to meet the expectations of nearly everyone all together. But the song does have a point, as it tells the story of a band who experienced big hits and fame, and that connects with an agent who left them high and dry by swindling away the copyrights of the songs that made them great. Perhaps in gaining fame, they were seduced by modernity and lost all they had created.

Interestingly, the church in America was struggling with its soul at the same time in the 1980s, emerging during the Reagan Revolution as the Moral Majority that would fully engage in the U.S. political establishment and begin down the road of supporting whichever Republican candidate happened to get nominated every four years. And just like the band's agent, every administration manages to trick the church out of what made it great in the first place—Jesus. The political establishment saw in the church an ally that could keep it in power and the church saw an ally that could protect it from the world's darkness. But as has been so often the case since Constantine co-opted the church in the third century, we just keep "looking for love in all the wrong places." And in doing so, generation after generation has to lose its soul all over again.

But the church has been defrauded by modernity in many ways other than just politics—by a capitalist culture that has infected the expectations of consumers in the pews, by an entertainment industry that demands fog machines and the very best rock and roll, by lite fare and menus such that sermons lack the depth to disciple that they once did.

In Deuteronomy 6, as the people are about to enter the promised land, God is concerned that the good life will co-opt them. He calls upon them not to forget who he is and what he has done for them. He encourages them to do whatever it takes to remember that he is God and that they are his people—to write it on their foreheads and doorposts—to tattoo themselves as it were so that they are constantly reminded of the allure of the culture around them. He wanted them to be vigilant about the temptations they were about to enter that could draw them away from their Creator and Redeemer and Protector.

I see the church as being far down river in this process of being co-opted by the larger society and culture and that going upstream will require the winds of the Holy Spirit. But in God's economy, which is anything but capitalistic or modern, it's never too late to turn our canoes around and head back toward the coming kingdom—a kingdom whose values, as my good friend Don Kraybill reminded us decades ago, are completely "upside down."

While my dad may have been a little over the top, I admire him now for being so vigilant about the world around us and its potential to open doors for us to be co-opted without even knowing. My parents saved me from a lot more than just movies of Goldie Hawn and Burt Reynolds that I'm no less for having missed. Thanks, Dad and Mom.

CHAPTER SEVEN

My Introductory Lecture in SOC 101, the Church, and Why It Is Not Working to Piece the Old Map Back Together

July 14, 2020

We are all born into a social map. We are dropped into this map, and none of us has any say over which map we land in. It's the fate of the divine card shuffle, and who of us can explain why we ended up on the map that we did. But the map that is ours makes all of the difference in where we end up in life. Because not all maps are created equal, nor are we all presented with the same set of paths for negotiating our social landscapes.

The religion or church we are born into also has a map, and is itself within a larger social map that includes our family, school, neighborhood, and so on. Since I am a Christian, I will specifically speak to Christian churches within the religious map of society. This map tells us lots of things. It contains statements about our beliefs— where we came from, why we exist, who God is, what is right and wrong, how to be successful in life, and on and on. This map also has a structure or organization. For Roman Catholics, this structure is quite hierarchical, and one always knows who is in charge, or at least that used to be the case. If you are Old Order Amish, the structure is much more egalitarian in nature, though there is still some hierarchy based on one's church leadership status, gender, and increasingly occupation. But there is about as much variety in structures of churches as there are churches.

Interestingly, when I consult with churches, I usually ask, "Where does authority lie in your structure?" Sometimes I put it more bluntly: "Who hires and fires the pastor?" It is incredible how few churches seem to know the answer to that question. When the response I get is "We don't know," I understand why I was called into the mess in the first place.

In any event, it is human to create structures, built by God into the design of our humanity and manifested early in creation through marriage and the family, followed by clans and tribes, etc. Structures are necessary because they provide the architecture by which we can live safely and securely without always keeping an eye out for who might hurt us next. Structures allow us to sleep at night.

Finally, every church or religious map includes rituals or social interaction. Ritual is repetitive, predictable (we know what to expect), and meaningful. The most significant of these rituals in the Christian tradition, from a theological perspective, is the Mass or Communion or Eucharist or Lord's table. This sacred ritual is central to the salvation narrative upon which the centuries of the church have been built and has meaning both for the individual and the corporate body of believers.

Baptism is, of course, right up at the top as well. So it should be no surprise that the Protestant Reformation involved some renovation of both, at least eventually, if not immediately, and at least in some parts of Christendom, if not all. Rituals, while meaningful, are not necessarily recognized as significant every time we do them. We may find ourselves bored with the Mass or with the homily or sermon or whatever. But take away rituals, and we suddenly recognize the loss we have experienced.

In this season of the Covid-19 crisis, which as I write, only shows signs of intensifying rather than losing momentum, we in the church now see in so many ways what we have lost. I talked with a friend who expressed frustration that church is not a church anymore, what with the social distancing between people and the masks and the lack of singing. "We just might not go back," he said. A friend shared with Heidi that they are not going back for the same reasons, to a church where singing and fellowship are strictly prohibited because of the need to distance themselves socially. "We can watch the sermon on our couch at home," she responded. And another group of leaders expressed that what was exciting the first Sunday as a remote congregation is now laden with heaviness.

Why? In large part because the map is gone. The culture of norms or unwritten rules has been severely damaged. We no longer know the rules of our gathering. I served as officiant in a wedding recently on the first day that our county was permitted re-gatherings, and it was clear that none of us knew the rules. The wedding coordinator came right up to me, put her hand on my shoulder, and got about six inches from my face. I knew things would be downhill from there. The groom's mother reached out to shake my hand and then apologized. Others came up to me and said, "You'll be brave enough to shake, won't you?" Okay, they didn't question my testosterone level explicitly, but I knew what they were saying covertly.

The point is—the rules are gone. Things are a mess. The structure is gone. Our own ministers are doing an incredible job of being creative, but how does one minister when the saints are gone, or all we can see of them is their lovely faces once a week looking at us. Or are they looking at their phone or just what are they doing? Sunday mornings, Heidi and I walk into the sanctuary, live stream the sermon, and go home. For a few weeks, I kind of enjoyed this because, you know, there was never the risk of getting sidelined by a saint concerned about the sermon. But now, I almost miss those conversations.

I suspect that the most significant reason our efforts to reassemble are so unsatisfactory is that they are efforts to remake the old map without doing so. We are creating something that resembles, try as we can, what was. But our every effort to do so simply reminds us that what was is no more. And so we end up grieving and missing the old but hating the new.

No, this is no way to recreate church. You can't add a mask and six feet to what was and expect to fool the saints. They are way too savvy for that—too many of them were already bored, and often rightfully so, without masks and when sitting shoulder to shoulder. The menu offered up on Sunday morning was often such light fare that the saints were already bailing out at a record rate in this country. Masks and six feet aren't bringing them back.

So what will? I don't have the answer except that I know a recreation of the old map is not the answer. The forms of church culture, structure, and ritual are constructed quite differently across cultures and evolve differently across time. The difficulty for us is that we didn't have time to evolve—suddenly, in February or March, we left the church. But we are finding that it is much more difficult to recreate than to shut down what we had. It is always more challenging to build than to destroy.

And yet the same God is sovereign over both tearing down and building up as he has made clear throughout all of history, whether it was his words to Noah after the flood or to Joshua entering a promised land that was full of dangerous inhabitants who would need to be cleared out first, or the early Jewish church that slowly began to recognize that the Holy Spirit was speaking to the Gentiles too.

I don't have the answers, but I do believe, at least for this evening, that the One who started this whole universe in the first place by the word of his mouth also has a fresh word for us, as to how we recreate a church that serves the purposes of the coming kingdom in a way that the old one did not. I keep coming back to where I so often do—this mess is the Spirit's doing, and the Spirit has been a Creator from the beginning, hovering over the chaos of the primeval deep and calling forth light and life. If God could do that then, at least a part of me believes he can do it again.

CHAPTER EIGHT

Life with God...From Terror and Torment to Peace and Prayer
July 16, 2020

I received an email recently from a listener who said this:

> Thank you so much for your podcast. I enjoy the perspective and wisdom of each of them—lots of fodder for thought and discussion. I have read through Psalms and now in Proverbs. One area I am having a challenge with is praying. I find it difficult because I feel I am not doing it correctly. It also feels insincere at times coming from me. I try to be thankful for the time and ask for guidance on my journey. I also ask for care and advice for loved ones, friends, and our problems now. I think I am doing ok, but I can't help but feel so trite. Any advice will be welcomed. Maybe a podcast subject. You have been a very important part of my return to Jesus.

I want to thank this individual for reaching out and identifying how this podcast has impacted their life with Jesus. At the end of the day, when the last episode is written, that more than anything is my prayer—that people would come to know the love of the One who created them and came to rid us of our shame and our blame and our pain and to assure us of his presence with us.

This question of how to pray is one that all of us must ask if we are serious about our life with God and knowing God. We know that the disciples of Jesus, who lived daily face to face with Christ, still felt the need to ask him how to pray. Maybe it was their observations of Jesus' own life with his Father that drew them into this question; perhaps it was the intimacy and authenticity of Jesus' life with the Father that they desired. Maybe it was their disgust with the pompous prayers of the religious leaders of the day who stood on the corners of streets pruning their feathers and strutting their religious goodness. Whatever it was, it is the same question that this listener is asking.

And that, my friend, is where we all must begin: "Lord, teach me to pray." Because I am convinced that God has created each of us with an internal spiritual ear capable of hearing his voice, and these spiritual ears are different from one person to another. You may ask me to read something or listen to a podcast that has meant so much to you, but when I hear it, it either makes no sense to me, or I find it discouraging or downright agitating. Why? Because we are hearing different things, filtered through the lenses of our life experiences, our personalities, but also perhaps our spiritual ears. For God did not create any of us the same, so why would we ever think we all hear God the same way.

No, God knows how you are created, and God knows best how you hear him. So beginning with this simple prayer of "Lord, teach me to pray" is precisely where we start. For God is waiting to teach us indeed how to hear him, how to listen for his voice—a voice that is constantly speaking to us but that until we become attuned to it, we will miss. And the first thing in beginning to tune into God's voice is to stop, be still, and "to know that he is God."

If there is one message that I want to be remembered for as a preacher, it is my continuous call for folks to develop a life with God. Their life with God will save them in crisis, in trouble, in sickness, in conflict, in pain. I tell them that in those moments, Heidi and I will be present with them, but there is only so much we can do to help them if they have not developed a life with God before the crisis. We would experience so much less pain if we took more seriously this little prayer: "Lord, teach me to pray. Teach me to hear you. Teach me to understand you and myself."

When I was a kid, I developed a regular devotional or quiet time with God from a very early age, perhaps around age 6 or 7. But my times were anything but quiet, what with the raging fears in my mind about my sins and possible damnation, asking God to forgive me over and over again, and leaving my time with God feeling worse than when I had started. I often felt like those times took me closer to hell than to heaven. I was legalistic, trying to have the perfect time with God. My Bibles from those early years have every verse underlined because I figured if I underlined one verse but failed to underline the others, I was elevating one verse above another. If it was all God's word, then every verse was equally valuable, and thus every verse should be underlined.

I spent much of my time with God confessing and re-confessing sins, but even by the end of this torturous exercise, I was still unconvinced that I was forgiven and I spent the rest of the day doing the same thing. Like I've said before, I don't know why I stayed with God when I began with a God who brought such trouble into my life.

The first change in my time with God occurred after Heidi and I separated early in our marriage. I was devastated by this loss and very alone; I knew only one thing to do—spend time with God. And so I did. I sat on our gold chair and read voraciously and journaled and cried out to God. The pain was so deep within me that the old terrors seemed less real and less present and less critical. They were mitigated to the back burner of my conscience while my heart began to drive my time with God in new ways. I read as much of the Desert Fathers as I could. I read the Catholic mystics. I abandoned almost everything evangelical because the theology of suffering among evangelicals is minimal to nonexistent. Instead we hear messages such as "Followers of Jesus are not to suffer, or if we do, we have failed, or if we want to be healed, we can send a $50 donation." But few evangelical authors have seen suffering as the seedbed for our healing and life and resurrection, which is so difficult for me to understand given that Jesus repeats again and again that death precedes life. All joy, all new life, comes as we walk through the death of the old life, and that old life only dies through suffering and experiences of brokenness.

My freedom from the torture of my earlier times with God occurred in part because of the rawness of my pain in that season, as I've said, but also because I was so broken and fractured that I didn't have the energy anymore to try to hold my life together, to pretend that I could get my prayers just right and perfect. No, I was so broken that the only thing I could pray was, "Jesus have mercy on me, a sinner."

And perhaps that's the second prayer for us to pray. If the first is "Lord, teach me to pray," a not so bad second is, "Lord have mercy on me, a sinner." Nothing moves the heart of God more, I suspect, than our recognition that we are so broken and damaged that we recognize only God can fix us, only God can heal us, only God can put us back together. The perfection of our prayers doesn't matter anymore. The only thing that matters to God is that we are close to him, that God holds us, that God loves us, that we are kept safe and secure in God's womb.

From this point on, my time with God became less fearful and something that I came to understand that I needed and relied upon as a single dad and full-time graduate student to help get me through one day after another during questions such as "How do I father my son? What if I can't get a job when I'm done with grad school? What if our marriage doesn't work out?" And on and on and on. God became a Father to me in those years in a way I had not experienced before. Broken and in despair, I finally began to hear God's voice to me through the din of my obsessive-compulsive nightmare.

A diagnosis of thyroid cancer that would lead to multiple surgeries and radioactive iodine treatments from 2000-2003 in our first stint of ministry was the second period when my life with God grew deeper, again because the terror of waking up each morning and wondering how long I had to live threw me into God's hands. I recognized that I had no other alternative. Or I did, but it was death and hell—and I had had enough of that in my quiet times earlier to know I didn't want to go back there. At this point in my life, the practice of getting up early before anyone else to meet with God developed and has continued—because I have come to recognize that I can't live without hearing God's voice, or at least I can't live well.

The third stage in the development of my life with God was my diagnosis of Parkinson's disease and the recognition that my life has a more apparent horizon to it than I had understood or recognized earlier, and that the only way I can "number these days aright" is to hear from God about my numbered days. Perhaps what has changed most in this season is my awareness that when I get up in the morning, God is already waiting for me, anticipating our time together. He is already prepared to give me the answers to the questions I have when I sit down with my cup of coffee. He is already there, and he is just delighted that you and I show up to spend time with him. Another thing that has changed is my recognition that my quiet time or devotions aren't a box to check off each morning but rather a way of being with God that stretches across my day. I'm not leaving God when I get up from my chair but instead starting my day with God and inviting God into that day—trying to tune my spiritual ears to hear him throughout that day. My time with God has led me to recognize that only a life with God will save me in the end. And I suspect that this is part of what Paul meant when he told us to pray continuously.

I am grateful for a spiritual director, Eldon Fry, who has encouraged me to practice sitting with God and sitting before God with my questions—sitting with my burdens—sitting with people who are on my heart. Sitting with God quietly and listening and resting and trusting, without pressure to get everything prayed that might need prayer, without pressure to get my prayers right, but simply being present to the God who loves me, created me, and knows how I hear him speak to me. In this way, prayer has become much less me talking to God and more of my listening for God.

But we don't get to the place of listening for God without suffering that drives us to God or without taking time to sit with God. Suffering and sitting—it was in this place that Job heard God and replied: "My ears had heard of you, but now my eyes have seen you." (Job 42:15 NIV)

CHAPTER NINE

*Those Whose Blood Runs Through
My Veins: Unifiers and Dismantlers,
Disrupters and Dividers, Priests and
Prophets—All Looking for a Better
Country, a Heavenly One*
August 1, 2020

About 15 years ago, Heidi and I left ministry at Elizabethtown Mennonite Church in what I would say some of the saints felt like was God's grace at work, and I have often said that I felt the same way. That I experienced leaving the ministry in that congregation as God's grace had much more to do with my struggles than with the dear saints we served. I found ministry to be the most challenging work I had ever done in my life. But then, I was diagnosed with papillary thyroid cancer just three months after my ordination and would struggle through multiple surgeries and treatments. I experienced nearly a lifetime limit of radiation until mercifully, one day following my third radioactive iodine treatment at Johns Hopkins, the disease suddenly decided, or God did, to back off to levels that for the most part have remained unthreatening though not in remission some twenty years since my diagnosis. For that, I am so grateful. We just celebrated our grandson Ezra Lee Kanagy's first birthday! I had not been sure that I would ever make it to see our son Jacob grow up.

The overt reason that we left congregational ministry was that I was called by my denomination at the time, Mennonite Church

USA, to survey its members and leaders, the results of which I framed within the context of the prophet Jeremiah. Interestingly, this prophet who was called both to tear down and build up, was the son of a priest named Hilkiah. I wonder how his father reacted to the tearing down or dismantling part of his young son's calling. Priests and pastors tend to be keepers of the status quo rather than movers and shakers, carrying out the traditions and rituals that create order, ensuring that things run smoothly from one generation to another. Yes, I suspect that Hilkiah's priestly vocation and his son's prophetic calling probably led to some interesting dinner conversations.

In my own blood, I have both prophets and priests running through the family generations. On both sides of my family, these prophets and priests are often remembered by folks whom I happen to bump into. "Oh, you are the grandson of Reverend Erie Renno" (my mother's father), long-time pastor at Locust Grove Mennonite Church who showed up at so many conflicted congregations and helped them put things back together. My much-loved Pap was a pastor who built up and who healed.

I wanted to be like Pap—known for his warm smile, his early innovations of doing away with the common Communion cup, and church council meetings before Communion when folks were sternly asked, "Are you at peace with God and your neighbor?" These rituals reinforced community bonds and brought with them a reminder that conformity to the community was at least every bit important, if not more than one's personal life with God. While the community brought with it strong accountability, rituals like these also have a way of diminishing honesty because who on any given day is entirely at peace with God and all our neighbors? If that's true of us, we must have died and gone to heaven, or else I alone am unusual in saying that complete peace with all of my neighbors and God, rarely if ever, describes me.

Pap was known for his significant emphasis on personal piety or intimacy with God rather than conformity to his community. To the end of his life, he had regrets about pastoral care decisions he had made that aligned with the community's expectation of conformity but crushed the life out of the individual that the decision affected. No, Pap had seen enough pain in the church to know better than to add to it. And for that, he is fondly remembered.

On my father's side, it is among the Kanagy's where the prophets tended to hang out. There seemed to be an entire band of these prophet brothers—dismantlers, dividers, destroyers. They were a restless bunch and often rough around the edges. My grandfather Norman left the Beachy Amish church for a Mennonite congregation in order, so I've been told, that he could adopt more progressive farming practices. He would then leave that Mennonite congregation decades later with a group of other restless folks in a problematic "split" (a word I soon learned as a kid meant terrible things that happened in church)—and would give them land on his farm to build a more conservative church. Before his death, he would be disillusioned again and leave that church for another.

My great uncle Ezra Kanagy (or Ed as he was also called) had his share of church troubles. Ordained as an Old Order Amish minister in Big Valley, he spent hours studying for his sermons, a rarity among Old Order preachers who typically share spontaneously as they preach. He studied the early Anabaptist writers and incorporated them into his sermons. He emphasized the assurance of salvation—that one could know beyond a shadow of a doubt that they belonged to Jesus as compared to a less confident "hope" for salvation that he heard his Amish brethren describe. His studies and his emphasis on personal salvation did not go well among the Amish in the Valley, and Ezra would find himself pitted against his in-laws, who were also church leaders as well as just about the entire Amish community. And so, he split—starting a New Order Amish congregation until it would eventually fizzle out within the strong culture of conformity in Big Valley. Uncle Ed moved to Shreve, Ohio, with a landscape less restrictive and family and church that received him for his emphasis on the peace that Jesus could bring.

In an interesting twist of fate, my grandfather Erie, the Mennonite pastor who brought unity, drove my Uncle Ezra, Amishman and more divider than unifier, to Harrisonburg, VA, to speak in chapel to the students of Eastern Mennonite University.

And then there was Uncle Lee, with his wife Adella, who served in Japan in the mid-20th century as missionaries and whom late in life grieved what he perceived to be the apostasy of the modern Mennonite church, so much so that he would go one way to his church on Sunday mornings and Adella to another. His brother Uncle Jake shared this pattern of going one way Sunday morning while his wife went another.

I am not criticizing these Kanagy brothers—simply pointing out the restlessness and "tearing down" attitude they sometimes expressed concerning the church. In the end, most of them left Big Valley and the church life they experienced there—even their parents did so, moving to Stuarts Draft, VA, late in life. I once heard someone in the family say that the Kanagys left the valley to escape church problems. And I'm sure that was partly true. But dismantlers, dividers, and destroyers are more complex than that—they are not cowards, nor do they run from difficulty. They don't buy the status quo that things are what they appear to be. They can only live with that dissonance so long, and if the cultural context in which they live won't budge, their life with God depends on them getting out as quickly as possible, knowing their salvation may depend on doing so.

It's easy to dismiss the dismantlers, the dividers, the destroyers. They've got problems, we say. They can't get along with anybody.

They are never satisfied. They are mentally ill. They are hard-headed. But when I read Hebrews chapter 11 about those restless saints on the run, it is pretty clear they were on the run to glory. Says the author:

> By faith Abraham obeyed when he was called to set out for a place that he was to receive as an inheritance; and he set out, not knowing where he was going. By faith he stayed for a time in the land he had been promised, as in a foreign land, living in tents, as did Isaac and Jacob, who were heirs with him of the same promise. For he looked forward to the city that has foundations, whose architect and builder is God. By faith he received power of procreation, even though he was too old—and Sarah herself was barren—because he considered him faithful who had promised. Therefore from one person, and this one as good as dead, descendants were born, "as many as the stars of heaven and as the innumerable grains of sand by the seashore." All of these died in faith without having received the promises, but from a distance they saw and greeted them. They confessed that they were strangers and foreigners on the earth, for people who speak in this way make it clear that they are seeking a homeland. If they had been thinking of the land that they had left behind, they would have had opportunity to return. But as it is, they desire a better country, that is, a heavenly one. Therefore God is not ashamed to be called their God; indeed, he has prepared a city for them. (Hebrews 11:8-16 NIV)

It's not easy to be the dismantler, the divider, the destroyer, the disrupter, but it is the prophetic office that some are given. Though often misunderstood, they are precisely the ones that the author of Hebrews is describing in these verses, tearing down so that they and others can excavate that highway to Mount Zion of Isaiah 40—lowering the mountains of bondage and slavery and imprisonment to conformity that stifles one's life with God, and raising the valleys where shame and guilt have been our closest allies, but in the light of God seeing them as the false narratives they are.

I'm grateful for those saints of Hebrews 11 who have gone on before us. And I'm thankful also for those in my own family tree who heard God's call and lowered mountains and raised valleys long before I showed up on the scene. I'm grateful for the priests and the prophets on both sides—even though I find that when the two show up together within me, sorting out which is which and which to listen to takes a lot more wisdom than I have. And yet, they are within all of us—and somehow, I suspect, living patiently in the tension is the only way to hear God's voice above the din of those saying "Do it our way" and others saying "No, do it this way. Do it the old way. No, do it the new way. You are doing it wrong. No, you are doing it right."

CHAPTER TEN

"Get Off the Road, You Slow Dutchman," and My Apology to That Dutchman— Uncle Ed Kanagy
August 1, 2020

Heidi and I just celebrated the first birthday of our grandson Ezra Lee Kanagy, or Ez as we sometimes call him. A bundle of joy and a gift from God, his first name in Hebrew means "Yahweh helps," while Lee (the middle name of the last four generations of firstborn Kanagy sons) means "to me." Yahweh helps me. Ezra came to us just in time—I need that reminder of Yahweh's help every day of this Covid-19 existence.

Growing up in Big Valley, where virtually all of us who were Mennonite had originated from the Amish who settled the valley in the late 18th century, we had this way of talking in stereotypical and stigmatized language about the Old Order Amish. It is comical and sad in retrospect, since we all had Amish relatives, and our ancestry was completely Amish, so it was kind of like standing at a mirror and mocking ourselves. And perhaps that is what we were doing. Maybe we never got over the trauma of leaving a society where conformity is so powerful that walking away from it means social death. Maybe saying "Dumb Dutchman" was our way of wrestling with our regret, rage, hurt, and pain that came with growing up in a small valley with one of the most schismatic Amish and Mennonite communities that any 45 square miles in the U.S. could have. It would take several lifetimes for a sociologist to figure out all that division—perhaps that is why so few have tried.

One sunny afternoon I was hurriedly driving up the valley, which we locals call going south even as the major stream that runs through the valley goes north. I had just driven by the Locust Grove Mennonite Church, where I worshipped every Sunday and had learned how I was to behave in situations like the one I was about to encounter. But I forgot my religious upbringing, as I saw a buggy in front of me with a lone Amishman who wouldn't get off the road. So muttering to myself, I flew around him and cut in as closely as possible to let him know just how agitated I was with his unwillingness to move off the highway.

But I made one mistake: I turned around. And when I did so, I could see that the Amishman was none other than my great Uncle Ed, the lone remaining Kanagy of his family who was both Amish and still living in the valley. Of all the possibilities of Amish men, it would have to be Uncle Ed at that moment and at that time.

I drove home. I had learned from my dad that taking care of our sins sooner rather than later was always best even if difficult. And so, I got into my car, and with my heart beating hard in my chest, drove to Uncle Ed's chicken house and walked up to him and said, "Uh, Uncle Ed, I'm sorry, but that was me who cut you off down on Rt. 655." "I know" was all he said. And probably all that needed to be said. We both knew well that in our little valley, your sins would find you out sooner or later.

It's always a bit hard to know our motives for apologies. Was I sorry that I cut off an Amishman or that the Amishman was Uncle Ed? To what degree was my apology about my embarrassment? Would I do things differently next time if I saw clearly that it wasn't Uncle Ed? Who knows. I'm just glad that when I ask Christ to forgive my sins and failures and my missing the mark, he compassionately and mercifully does so.

What I didn't know at the time was that of all the Kanagy brothers in my grandfather's family, Ed was probably the one with which I had the most in common. He suffered torment as I did, trying to discover an assurance of his salvation with God. Ed would preach, against the will of the Amish leadership, that we can know Jesus intimately and know that someday we will be with Jesus. My preaching has gotten me in trouble as well.

But Ed was also a writer and a historian, a scribe for several national Amish newspapers. He wrote more than history, though. He wrote about nature and farming and the beauty of life. Like the others of this rough and tumble band of Kanagy prophets, Ed wrote with an honesty and vulnerability so unlike what the culture of the valley generally permitted. And perhaps that is what ultimately contributed to his leaving for Ohio, where he would live out his remaining days with Parkinson's disease.

Dismantler and prophet, one who wrestled with finding intimacy and an authentic life with God, a writer with vulnerability and transparency, and finally a fellow sufferer of the all-encompassing disease that I too have been diagnosed with.

But Uncle Ed lived a full life, a beautiful life, and a life with God. Having a grandson named Ezra Kanagy, it is hard not to remember and be grateful for Uncle Ed.

CHAPTER ELEVEN

Uncle Alvin Kanagy—Baby of the Family But a Giant in the Faith

August 2, 2020

Uncle Alvin was the baby of the fourteen Kanagy children of Jacob and Salina—my great-grandparents who left the valley late in life. Rumor has it that in part it was to escape the religious oppression of the place. As I recall, Alvin carried that stigma of being the youngest all of his years. We all carry such stigmas—they are held over our heads for whatever reason by others—sometimes malicious and sometimes benign, but they continually shape and form us. Sometimes we cave into them, and sometimes their very existence creates a fierce resistance within us to show others that we are anything but what they think we are.

I didn't know Uncle Alvin any better than the other uncles, but I knew and heard enough to know that he and his family had lived a kind of missionary existence in West Virginia, where Alvin served as a pastor. They didn't have much in the way of material goods, and sometimes brothers from the valley would take things down to support them. My dad tells of my grandfather Norman driving to West Virginia to present Brother Alvin with a new truck.

But while the other brothers were often ramblers, dismantlers, dividers, rough around the edges, and more prophets than priests, I always knew Uncle Alvin for how much he looked out of place in that crew. He was, it seemed to me, as much the gentle and kind pastor as my Pap Erie Renno. Uncle Alvin seemed settled. His face was always kind. I remember him for the warmth of his smile and eyes that lit up at the same time. But then there was that stigma that he would again joke about if someone else didn't beat him to it.

The baby of the family or not, Alvin was no baby in his life with God. His face and eyes also carried the intensity and seriousness of one who has been tempted and tried and has figured out who God is and what God requires of us. His faith had been tested, and in the summer of 1991, at a Kanagy reunion in Mifflin County, Alvin would share the Sunday morning message. And I was all ears. My wife Heidi and I had separated the summer before, and I was desperate for a word of hope.

Nearly a decade later, in the summer of 2000 at that year's Kanagy Reunion, I was asked to give the morning message—nine years after Alvin had done so. During this period, he had passed away. I could not attend the reunion because I had been diagnosed with papillary thyroid cancer just three weeks before and was recovering from surgery. But still, I wanted to share, and so I wrote out the message and gave it to my parents to present for me. Here is an excerpt:

> To those who are gathered for the 2000 reunion of the Jacob and Salina Kanagy family, I greet you in the name of Christ, the one about whom C. S. Lewis noted that "for those who remain in him, nothing much can ever go wrong." That phrase was the bottom line of a message I delivered to our congregation one week ago. "Nothing can go wrong with those who remain in Jesus?" Lewis must have been half-mad to have made such a shocking statement. In response to Lewis, and perhaps for my own doubt more than for the congregation, I reinforced the words of Lewis with those of St. John, a saint who knows, if any of us do, about things gone wrong in the world. "For everyone born of God overcomes the world. This is the victory that has overcome the world, even our faith." (I John 5:4 NIV)

John's message is so simple. If we are in Jesus, we will over-come the world. Simple, straightforward, uncomplicated. It's a message that Martin Luther comforted us with five centuries ago when he said that "When we are in Christ we have every-thing. But we have also lost everything when we no longer are in Christ. So cling to Christ, when your eyes do not see him and your ears do not hear him, and your senses do not feel him."

And it was a simple message that I heard at the Kanagy reunion at this same place nine years ago, when I came as a graduate student at Penn State, a single father, no idea of what lay ahead, in tremendous debt, no career plan, and a marriage in tatters. In that context I found myself at a Kanagy reunion on a Sunday morning much like this one.

Uncle Alvin spoke that morning. And what he said, I will never forget. Since then, his message has stayed with me and has been a constant reminder that Lewis, Luther, and St. John got it exactly right. "Nothing much can go wrong for those who are in Christ." Alvin gave testimony to how God had faithfully, time upon time, provided for him and his family. I can't remember any of the details. I can't remember any of the words. I only remember with my heart what Alvin said that morning: "Jesus cares for us. When we walk with Jesus, He will walk with us, and He will take care of us." Alvin's life and testimony that morning so clearly showed the faithfulness of God's love for his people.

In closing, Alvin himself noted that he didn't know the future as he approached retirement and the uncertainties of aging and health. And those of us here this morning know that those uncertainties caught up with Alvin as they have now with so many of the original clan of Kanagys. And yet, I suspect that Alvin continued to claim the promises he shared with us on that Sunday morning.

In any event, I walked out of the reunion that morning with a simple challenge to believe that everything was going to be well—not because I could verify it but because the truth of God had been expressed in the life of another child of God. And so I come back to tell you this morning, more sorry than you can know that I am not with you in person. But I come back to say to you that Alvin is right. Luther is right. Lewis is right. And St. John is right. I have come back to join Uncle Alvin these years later in saying simply that Jesus loves us. He cares about us. And as we walk in him, he meets the needs that we have. It's that simple.

And that's about all I shared that morning, but the experience reminds me of just how critical it is for those of us who love Jesus to express that love to our children. Teaching them to believe in Jesus will only go so far if they don't see that we have a life with Jesus. But if we have developed a life with Jesus, the words will go a lot further because they will magnify what our children see in us.

While this message was from 2000, the last twenty years have brought more challenges. I would struggle for three years with that particular cancer diagnosis. Then Heidi was diagnosed with ovarian cancer in 2008. I fell off the roof and broke my hip in 2013, was diagnosed with salivary gland cancer in 2014, and was diagnosed with Parkinson's disease in 2017. In between, Heidi and I had numerous struggles in our congregational ministry that we sometimes thought would take us under.

But by now, there is no turning back. I've thrown my chips in with Jesus. I look forward much more than I look back. I see a horizon now with my Parkinson's diagnosis that I did not see so clearly before. But it is helping me to number my days a little better, I think, and to enjoy the good gifts of God a bit more. And it has helped me to decide to tell my story in a way I never have before, because our stories are of his story—of his faithfulness and goodness and love. If Uncle Alvin hadn't been willing to share his story that Sunday morning, this young single dad with little to no hope just might have washed out. But Alvin's faith built up my faith. And I say with him now, these twenty years later—Uncle Alvin, you are one of my heroes of faith no less than those of Hebrews 11. The baby you might have been in your family of origin, but a giant of faith in the kingdom of God you became. Thank you for passing that faith onto me in a most challenging season of my life.

CHAPTER TWELVE

Changed Diagnosis and Prognosis and a Full Belly Laugh
August 7, 2020

I do not believe that God always heals us of our diseases or that followers of Jesus will never suffer or that we won't die with some questions we would like to ask God about. But I do suspect that given what the new heaven and new earth promise us, the questions will disappear about as soon as we show up in that new Eden.

At the same time, I have a hunch that if we were quiet long enough, all of us might remember some experience in our lives, at least one, where the diagnosis or prognosis was suddenly turned upside down. And for just a moment or two we wondered if there might be a deity who cares about our existence after all. I'd encourage you to go back and spend a little time thinking about that time again, as we are in the middle of a season where we could use another experience just like that.

There have been several such times for Heidi and me. In April 2000, three months after my ordination as Lead Minister of Elizabethtown Mennonite Church, I was diagnosed with papillary thyroid cancer. This cancer is usually quite treatable with surgery and radioactive iodine. The challenge, however, was that my tumor had already reached five centimeters—I was only 35 years old—and these factors immediately affected my long-term prognosis. I had surgery and got through my first radioactive iodine treatment—a treatment we had every reason to believe I would never need again.

A year later, a follow-up to my endocrinologist revealed levels of thyroglobulin that suggested a recurrence of the disease, but imaging didn't reveal where it was located. Doing some of my own research, I sought a second opinion. The surgeon took one look at the same images and pointed directly to the diseased lymph nodes that accounted for the earlier test results indicating disease.

I underwent surgery and another radioactive iodine treatment at a new hospital with a new surgeon and endocrinologist. And the following summer, bloodwork revealed continued disease. I had a third radioactive iodine treatment and was approaching what was considered a lifetime limit of radiation. Indeed, test results the following year again suggested ongoing disease. I asked for imaging, however, before a fourth and likely final treatment. In an appointment with Dr. Ball, my endocrinologist, his demeanor was serious as he noted that I was now an outlier and the path ahead was not entirely clear anymore. So I withdrew from my thyroid replacement medication one more time—a withdrawal required for the test and that always resulted in packing on more pounds as my metabolism slowed to a halt.

As I lay on the table in preparation for the scan, I prepared for the worst. As I came out of the scan, I looked at the monitor and, for the first time, unlike previous tests, I did not see the black spots that had lit up in areas of disease. I knew that another patient was being tested ahead of me, so I assumed that what I saw on the monitor was the result of his scan. As the tech approached me, he smiled: "I don't think we will see you again." I didn't know what to think but assumed one of two things—the disease was gone, or it was so bad that this was indeed my last trip to Johns Hopkins and I was at the end of the road.

It turns out, in a few minutes, Dr. Ball would confirm that "there is no longer any evidence of disease." I walked to the parking lot and let out a full belly laugh I will never forget—life had been given back to me at the most unexpected time, at a time when I had just finished the book of Job and with Job had said, "Alright God, I hear you, you are more significant than I ever was or will be. Do as you wish with me."

So what does one say? Things often don't always turn out this way, and sometimes they won't for us again either. Folks are praying that my Parkinson's disease will disappear. It may or may not. I'm doubtful even though I believe all things are possible with the One who made all things. What I do know is that God is merciful and sometimes that mercy is displayed in changing diagnoses and prognoses, and other times that mercy is displayed in giving us just enough light to get to the new heaven and earth—for some sooner than later.

But I suspect that all of us who stumble across the thin veil between the darkness and chaos and violence of this earth into the full sunshine and blue sky of the next will never look back and consider it anything less than his mercy that he called us Home when he did.

So what does this mean for we who are in one way or another exiles on earth these days, awaiting our Home that lies just over the horizon? I'm not sure. Except that I do remember Jeremiah 29, and that crazy prophet with truth burning in his bones who called up the exiles in Babylon. Fortunately for them, they took his call one more time.

"I know this might sound crazy," it is possible Jeremiah prefaced, "but God says party on! Have kids. Buy homes. Marry off those kids. Have grandkids. But don't forget that you are a people of shalom even while in exile. So seek the peace and prosperity of those around you, pagan or not, because if you do, peace and prosperity will always party with you."

The problem for those of us in exile is that it is so easy to believe that God has rejected us, and the more we languish in that, the more likely we are to believe that we deserve his rejection. And the longer we hang out in rejection, the more likely we are to reject him back and also to forget that there is anything good about us that the world so desperately needs.

And so we become exiles with the short view—focused on accumulating, protecting, squatting down, and forgetting the marginalized and the oppressed. "Come on," says Jeremiah, "not only are you to party on, your God hasn't forgotten you but has plans to prosper you and not harm you, plans to give you hope and a future."

And so exile, wherever you are, whoever you are, and whatever you are running from, let's get up off our duffs in the middle of the Covid-19 nightmare, have a party, and invite our neighbors. Just don't forget to wear a mask and social distance. And remember, wherever shalom shows up, God is present.

CHAPTER THIRTEEN

The Lord's Table From Sacrament to "Symbol"—What the Low Church Lost in the Last Dismantling

August 15, 2020

I'm hearing two different voices these days about the future of the church. On the one hand, I've listened to some scholars of church history argue that the church has always found a way to assemble, and we can be confident that the church will continue to exist. As a result, let's continue planning for the future as if the church will be the same as it was pre-Covid-19.

On the other hand, I am also hearing from the saints in the pew that the "churchless" life we are leading is getting to be relatively comfortable, with the gathering of the saints becoming a bygone era and virtual sainthood increasingly attractive, a postmodern kind of sainthood that means, well, like most things postmodern—not much.

Being one of those in the low church, free church, believers' church, true church, or whatever else we have called ourselves since the Radical Reformation took Luther and Calvin's reforms to a new level, I am struck by how few calls I hear for the sharing of the Lord's Table or Communion or whatever your church calls it. In fact, in a survey of our congregation and what they have missed since we stopped assembling, not one mentioned baptism, Communion, feet-washing (which, if we are honest, we gave up a long time ago because it just isn't modern or post-modern). In fact, it has only been within the last week that I started thinking about how much I miss Communion, telling Heidi, "I'm going to find a Eucharist service somewhere—I have to meet Jesus at his table."

Since giving up the sacraments five hundred years ago, believing as we did that they are not actually saving graces after all but simply water, bread, and grape juice, we have sufficiently downplayed them along with a host of other things in the high church tradition such as saints and relics and icons and statues and stained glass windows and high ceilings and just about anything else that might move the heart and soul toward the mysteries of God.

We retained, or so we thought, the preaching of the Word and the body of believers. But Communion or the Lord's Supper and baptism we relegated to the order of symbols, and in doing so suggested to our children that symbols, while important, are not all that meaningful. Which, of course, is not true. As human beings, we live and die by the symbols we embrace—the flag, our currency, the consumer labels on our clothing, the Bible, our vehicles, language, and so much more. Is there anything else that we tell our children is a symbol without meaning?

Children, here is a Philadelphia Eagles jersey for you, but it doesn't really mean anything. Here is a Christmas gift that we know you wanted, and it is a symbol of our love, but it doesn't mean anything. Dear fiancé, will you marry me? Here is a diamond ring, but I just want to clarify that the diamond is meaningless. We have basically said that compared to our high church brothers and sisters who worship the host (bread at Mass), we actually worship Jesus. But what we have done is to take power out of the Lord's Table and out of baptism and out of every other sacrament from which we have stripped meaning and called a symbol. Just a tad bit arrogant, I think.

Maybe I was the only kid who heard this stuff growing up— but it felt like it was drummed into my head by the church, and in fact, I have passed it on to others myself. What have I passed on? You know, the idea that the Lord's Table is just symbolic but has no saving power. Folks, we are wrong about this—what we have done is to neuter the power of these symbols that Jesus pleaded with us to continue practicing until he returns. Sounds like they had some meaning to Jesus. In fact, in one Gospel he told his disciples that "I can't wait to have this Last Supper with you." Why? Because the love of God was going to be revealed in a way the world had never seen before as they sat around that floor together that night and broke the body of Christ and drank his blood.

Growing up, I heard that we had Communion twice a year as Mennonites because we didn't want to get bored or too used to it or allow it to become a tradition, lest in doing so it would lose all meaning. Which if you think about it makes no sense because we had just been taught that it was really not all that meaningful anyway. Frankly, I think we were perplexed and have been for the last 500 years about exactly what happens at the Lord's Table and baptism.

But this argument never made sense to me. We never said let's eat twice a year, so we don't get bored with it or lest we make eating an idol (which, of course, the smorgasbord and giant buffet took care of for us all). I never heard it suggested that we restrict couples to making love twice a year, so they don't get bored with it and decide to divorce because they've got too much intimacy. I never learned that it is important to watch NFL football games just twice a season so that we don't lose interest in watching grown men draw blood. No, we know that we do those things with the most value and meaning as often as we can. What we love, we do. What we love, we buy. Why do we show such incredible discipline when it comes to the Lord's Table?

Not only did I not buy the argument, I believed that the Lord's Table was to be feared because I heard sermon after sermon that this was the case. If you drink this cup unworthily, you will lose your soul. But wait a minute, you just told me that Communion has no power to save me, but now turn around and say it can damn me if I do it all wrong. And perhaps that is the real reason we Anabaptists relegated Communion to twice a year—we were scared to death of the Lord's Table's power to damn because we had long given up on its power to save. Like the Amish, we practiced the bi-annual council meeting before Communion in which folks were asked whether they were at peace with God and their neighbor. Among the Amish today, a negative answer can stall Communion. So who in their right mind is going to be stigmatized for being out of peace with God and our neighbor though in fact most of us are every day of the year. In fact, this is precisely why Jesus came—so that we could confess that we are not at peace and be forgiven for this rather than be penalized, stigmatized, and kicked out until we get our act together.

While our congregation did not practice council meetings, as my grandfather had done away with them, I think the residue re-mained from our centuries-old history of treating a symbol as if it had no meaning but all the while replacing it with fear of damnation and hellfire—always a perfected trick of the devil himself. Before Communion each time, I would literally sweat and shake that I was about to take the bread and the cup unworthily and that on my way back to my pew might just die for having done so. The entire way up the aisle, I would ask for forgiveness of all my sins until the bread and grape juice were running down the back of my throat. And I breathed a sigh of relief when I made it back to my seat without fall-ing into the fiery pit.

While this may sound extreme, it was truly my experience, and it would be decades before I would preach that we come to this table to meet Jesus not because we are perfect but because we are so imperfect. We come to this table because we need Jesus so badly and not because we don't. We come to this table because we don't have the power to be at peace with God and our neighbor and not because we do. I come to this table because my life depends on it. And if there is no meaning in that, I'm not sure where to find it.

In this moment of Covid-19, our high church friends at least have the advantage of being able to get their folks to come to church to receive the host, which then creates a context where they also happen to run into each other after they've run into Jesus. But in the free church, low church, believers' church, true church, or whatever else we call ourselves, we have lost this advantage because we have downplayed and minimized the Lord's Table or Communion, historically relegating it to just a few times a year and suggesting, if implicitly, that it is not really that important after all. So we have one less reason to gather these days—because we don't believe that there is anything mysterious or powerful about the cup and the bread. But I do—I need it desperately.

And so I don't know about you, but it's way past time for me to find a table where the Lord is waiting for me, and I'm not going to wait until we reassemble to do so. I'm coming, Jesus, and I can't wait to join you there.

CHAPTER FOURTEEN

When God Says "No" to Your Will for Your Life But "Yes" to What Will Give You Life

August 22, 2020

O ur lives are full of twists and turns, steps forward and back-ward, sometimes near misses, and occasionally total head-on collisions. When I was a kid, I was sure that a faithful Christian pre-pared to be a missionary. So that was precisely what I would do. For if your goal is to become a saint, even though you're pretty sure that's beyond your paygrade, you do what you have to do. So a missionary I would become. I read books by missionaries. I visited with mission-aries after they shared on Sunday evenings at our church, and I asked them lots of questions. If I acted interested enough, sometimes they would give me an artifact or something else from wherever God had sent them in the world. But during my freshman year in high school, I began having severe back pain, so intense that some days I couldn't tie my shoes, and I chronically wore a back brace. It turns out I had spinal stenosis at an early age and the surgeon told me that I should never plan on having a career in manual labor.

Two summers later, I would go with an organization called Team Missions International for one summer in Honduras, another in the Dominican Republic, getting trained, of course, to be a mission-ary. And I already decided the kind of missionary that I would be—a missionary pilot. It sounded exciting, not particularly threatening for an introvert who knew he should tell people about Jesus but wanted to run away at about every opportunity that he had to do so.

In fact, I had joined a very small group of folks from church who would do door-to-door evangelism. I was the only kid who participated, and I am sure they thought I had a particular zeal for the Almighty, but what they didn't know was that I was just trying to stay on the Almighty's good side in preparation to be a missionary. I wasn't sure that the Four Spiritual Laws (the tract we distributed) were the good news that everyone cracked them up to be, for how could the Gospel really be about four laws? Hadn't Jesus come to overcome the law with his grace? Could human beings mess up the good news any more than that?

But I assumed that I needed to keep at it, not only to get myself into heaven, but because this is what missionaries in training were supposed to do. And the fact that missionary life didn't seem like much fun to me was beside the point. Because dying to self meant you had to go to Africa or wherever God sent you, no matter whether you wanted to or not. But in one of those summers with Teen Missions, I learned that missionary pilots actually had to do a lot of manual labor. Aware that I couldn't do that, I would have to find another way to be a missionary. For it was clearly God's will for my life. And for everyone else, too.

With my pre-determined calling in mind, in 1982, I went to Wheaton College, a level of culture shock I was not prepared for but eventually came to grips with and actually thrived during my four years there. They were the most significant years of my spiritual formation up to that point in my life. In my first year, I decided to major in Religious Studies or Bible in order to prepare for the mission field.

But when the time came during my freshman year to declare a major, I backtracked after some struggle and decided I could always go to seminary after college. I should have some cross-cultural training as an undergraduate student. So an anthropology/sociology major I became for the sole purpose of becoming a missionary.

But I struggled to get excited about my courses in those first few years. One day, my advisor Dr. Dean Arnold sat me down and looked me in the eye and said, "Conrad, if you don't get focused or excited about something, you're not going to make it." But I was going to be a missionary, and I had no idea that excitement was a prerequisite. It was simply obedience and doing the right thing that counted.

In my junior year, I was introduced to sociological research by Dr. Ivan Fahs, and I came alive academically for the first time. I suddenly found a passion that kept me up in the department lab at night, running data, writing papers, and hanging out with the academic nerds. But how in the world was this newfound passion going to fit with being a missionary? For one thing, I was having fun. Second, I was thriving, successful in winning state and regional writing awards. Third, I had an excellent mentor in Dr. Jim Mathisen. He saw potential I had never seen or allowed myself to see. Because when God tells you you're going to be a missionary, you don't spend time imagining other possibilities or dreaming of other worlds. Doing so lacks the kind of discipline required in missionary preparation. Right? You know, you discipline yourself not to dream of other possibilities. Not to imagine different things outside of what you sense God calling you to do.

But Dr. Mathisen saw things I couldn't believe in dreaming of and other worlds for me that I didn't even know existed. As the deadline for one of the undergraduate writing competitions approached, I went to Blanchard Hall one day prepared to inform Dr. Mathisen that I would not be able to finish the paper in time. But as I started to tell him this, he didn't blink or miss a beat. He just handed me another draft with red ink all over it and said, "Nope," with a sly grin, "you are going to finish and meet the deadline in time." What was I to say? Of course, I did finish the paper, and received an award in the competition. And Dr. Mathisen took me to my first professional sociology conference in Des Moines, Iowa, where my heart and mind began to see a world I didn't know existed.

And then, it came time to graduate, and I had always planned on going to seminary. But the preceding year had shown that I was actually pretty good at sociology, and with the help of Dr. Mathisen, my writing continued to improve. So what was I to do? I struggled. I ruminated. I hemmed and hawed. Why would God call me to be a missionary and then allow me to experience so much joy in my sociology work? Was my success simply a demonic temptation or test to leave the straight and narrow path? Or had I missed hearing God's voice all along through the years? If I had missed his voice in this, where else had I missed his voice? In the end, it was probably the intensity of the struggle that, in part, kept me from doing justice to my search for graduate schools.

At the last minute, I applied to the University of Pittsburgh in anthropology, and received an assistantship. I went the following Fall. Despite success, I experienced one of my most challenging years ever with the mental and emotional struggles that had persisted all of my young life. I finally left early at the end of the first year, diagnosed with a severe case of mononucleosis. Was this God's way of dealing with my disobedience and not going to seminary and instead choosing what I loved?

Time would tell, but the hard knocks continued. And for quite a while, things looked pretty bleak. Dropping out of graduate school, I took a job as an auto battery salesman, Heidi and I married, and then separated less than two years after the birth of our son. No, it didn't seem much like God was rewarding the choices I had made.

After Heidi and I had married in March 1988 and after we became aware that Heidi was pregnant with Jacob, I decided to try graduate school again. The tragedy was that I didn't have a conversation with Heidi about this decision. And I would reap the consequences of that later. But amid this, God was also at work.

Even though it was May, and I knew that the chances of receiving an assistantship and tuition remission for the rapidly approaching academic year were likely over by this point, I made an appointment to see the chair of the Department of Rural Sociology at Penn State. I pulled my white auto battery van onto the campus, then walked into the department office. I shook hands with the department chair as he invited me to sit down. "I'm Dr. Donald Crider, the Interim Chair of the Department this year. I'm a Wheaton College graduate and a United Methodist minister. Because we gave so many assistantships out one year ago, we actually did not admit any incoming graduate students this year. And so it turns out that I think we might just have enough money to offer you a package allowing you to come in August, paying for your tuition and providing an assistantship with a stipend and health insurance."

What does one say in a moment like that? When God reveals that God was leading all along, and that the detours we experienced were actually the exact route God had us on, and where what appeared as the most direct route might actually have ended in a full head-on collision. St. Paul says after all that God does this kind of thing—works all things out for the good of those who love him. In the short term, this truth is so hard to see, but in the long term, and for some experiences only from the perspective of eternity, the truth of this promise is revealed. For the God who restores all things, never stops working on our behalf or on behalf of the world that he so loved and so loves us still, and someday, that will be clear to all of us.

CHAPTER FIFTEEN

Leaders Who Plan for Their Assassination and a Grandfather Who Had the Wisdom to Prepare for His Descent Into Death

November 8, 2020

I woke early one morning this week and grabbed a book that a friend had recently recommended by Andy Crouch, entitled *Strong and Weak: Embracing a Life of Love, Risk and True Flourishing*.[4] I found this book a very insightful read about leaders and the relationship between authority and vulnerability. Leaders who are vulnerable and lead with appropriate authority create a space where people can flourish.

I was particularly struck by what Crouch said about the need for leaders to prepare for the end of their tenure. In doing so he cites the work of Ronald Heifetz and Marty Linsky who in their book *Leadership on the Line,* argue that leaders must prepare for their own assassination. Leaders must have the wisdom to choose when and how they descend from their positions of power. They must be ready to "descend to the dead" by giving up authority. If they cannot or will not do so they are nothing less than a dictator.[5] Crouch reminds us that effective leaders plan for their exit before their own communities often do so. Failure to make such plans is destructive for any

---

[4]   Andy Crouch, *Strong and Weak: Embracing a Life of Love, Risk and True Flourishing* (Downers Grove, IL: IVP Books, 2016).

[5]   Ronald Heifetz and Marty Linsky, *Leadership on the Line: Staying Alive through the Dangers of Leading* (Boston: Harvard Business School Press, 2002).

community left in the wake of that leader. Both leaders and their community must plan for the transition that will inevitably occur.

Leadership as pastors, parents, presidents, and more is not for our own benefit but for the benefit of those we lead. And the more we assume we are necessary to the whole enterprise, the greater the pain when we eventually realize that we have not prepared for our assassination and have resisted the vulnerability of being a human being. For the exit from a leadership role is one of the richest times of insight and growth for the leader who exits with his or her eyes open. It is only in backing out the door into the unknown that we finally see where we were, what we were up to all along, where we succeeded and where we failed. But too many of us deny that transition because we fear what we might see if we were actually to choose to go through the exit door, where our descent into death requires that we be vulnerable about our own humanness. While vulnerability isn't something we're so comfortable with in our culture, death always reveals it.

I told a friend this week that the tremors I experience when I feel stress make it uncomfortable sometimes to be in my own body. This friend reminded me that the value of the tremors is that I can't hide my humanness anymore. My vulnerability as a leader is now front and center, which has also meant that I'm reminded every day that my body slowly but undoubtedly faces its own dismantling and that I better prepare for my own descent into the dead. And most days I don't find this discouraging or depressing. This constant reminder has meant that I am more focused on what I want to do and what I don't, what I can do and what I can't, who I want to be with and who I won't, and so on.

On the eve of World War II, C. S. Lewis stated that "Human life has always been lived on the edge of a precipice and that if men had postponed the search for knowledge and beauty until they were secure, the search would never have begun."[6] It is in embracing our vulnerability as soldiers on the front lines, as leaders facing our own demise, or as stroke survivors that we come to recognize a beauty and grace and joy that we never experienced before. Perhaps preparing for our assassination and our descent into death isn't just wise, it might also lead to the most incredible beauty we can ever imagine.

My grandfather Erie "Pap" Renno, a longtime minister at Locust Grove Mennonite Church and an overseer in the Conservative Mennonite Conference, well in advance of his retirement, informed the congregation that no matter what his health was like, he would retire at 65 years of age. Too often he had been called to assist congregations where the conflict was related to older leaders who had hung on too long and created destruction and dysfunction as a result. He had no interest in doing so. At the top of his game and in excellent health, he kept his promise.

Pap went on to serve many years at a local retirement community as a deeply loved chaplain until he retired again, this time, he said, "because it just wasn't fun anymore." I love that statement. Pastors, parents, presidents, and all leaders, our time is short, and our influence limited and finite. It is better to leave at the top of one's game than to be assassinated because we overstayed our time. Choosing our own assassination, painful as it may be, will be a short-term cost for an eternal gain—for us and for the communities of faith that we lead.

---

[6]   C. S. Lewis, *The Essential C. S. Lewis* (New York, Scribner, 1996).

CHAPTER SIXTEEN

Why I Continue to Teach Sociology, the "Dark Side" of Society, and That Grand Excavation Project of Isaiah
August 26, 2020

In 2006 I began a research project for Mennonite Church USA, a project that was intended to be a follow-up to two other significant studies from 1972 and 1989 of Anabaptist-related denominations. I'm not sure what denominational leaders expected to learn, but to their credit, they took the risks that come with looking at themselves long and hard in the mirror. If they knew anything about sociology, they knew that we have a knack for looking under the floorboards of society, through the windows of homes, and in the basements and attics of whatever and whomever we are studying. We are never satisfied to read the propaganda from a congregation's website, its weekly bulletin, or some sanitized statement of centennial history. We are interested in the dirt in the corners of the Sunday School classrooms and the gossip by Board members in the parking lot.

Sociologists know that where there are people, there is dirt, and where there is dirt, there are treasures to be found. And so like the character who grabs his metal detector and heads out to the playground, park, or beach to find what no one else can see on the surface, so the sociologist insists on looking underneath what we call the "taken for granted reality," that stuff deep in the back of our brains that accumulates over time as we are socialized, and we never even think about it being there. For if we did stop and think about it, we would assume that what is in the back of our brains was arrived at in some rational way. As Peter Berger, one of my favorite sociologists, argues that "the first wisdom of sociology is this—things are not what they seem."[7]

As I began the denominational project, I took a day retreat to Big Valley, up in the mountains by what we always called Uncle Jake's shanty—a somewhat by now deteriorated hunting cabin in need of repair but all the more mysterious because it is so. Just below that cabin, at some point in the day, as I was praying for direction for the project, I distinctly heard what I believed then and believe now was God's voice, somehow pointing me to the book of Jeremiah, chapter thirty-one. I don't remember how it happened, but I found verse 21: "Set up road signs; put up guideposts. Take note of the highway, the road that you take...." (NIV)

I knew before too long that this verse, this command to the people of God as they returned from exile, was also the lens through which I was to interpret the data of the denominational profile I was leading. That somehow, this project, by virtue of the findings, was to offer a set of roadsigns to the church. And so I read prolifically the various authors who had written about the prophet Jeremiah and what he was up to. And as it turns out, he and I were up to similar things—trying to figure out what God was saying to God's people and what God wanted all of us to know about the mess we were in.

Because God's people then and God's people now were in severe and similar messes—abandonment of the poor and the marginalized and widows and orphans, sacrificing their children as the pagans did, spending their money on wealth and well-being, and

---

[7]   Peter Berger, *Invitation to Sociology* (New York: Doubleday: 1963), 23.

abandoning the Year of Jubilee when the land was to be redistributed to its original owners and slaves set free.

I analyzed the data that we received through the lens of the prophetic words of Jeremiah. I began to understand that Jeremiah was at least as much a sociologist as I was, and just perhaps a bit of the prophetic was getting under my skin as well. Because both sociologists and prophets perform similar functions: We look where others refuse to look, ask questions others refuse to ask, give answers that are usually unpopular, challenge the status quo, and are both seen as irreverent and sometimes sacrilegious. We call what some consider sacred as profane (or ordinary, every day) and what is considered profane as sacred. We are rarely appreciated in our lifetimes and only so once it appears that perhaps we knew what we were talking about after all.

Christian Smith, an evangelical Christian and well-known sociologist of religion from Notre Dame who has done substantial work related to evangelical youth culture, argues that the role of a sociologist is to examine the dark side of society, the underbelly of the worlds that we live in—those social realities that we deny, ignore, and cover-up until the next generation has no idea those parts ever existed.[8] Perhaps if we refuse, ignore and cover up the truth about our families, churches, universities, and other institutions, the truth will never come back to haunt us. But sociologists are the unveilers of that which is denied, ignored, and covered up. And for that, we are rarely appreciated.

The prophetic role of sociology was clear from its beginnings. Karl Marx, writing in Germany in the mid-19th century, predicted that the modern world and the industrial revolution would evolve such that human beings would become alienated from one another, from their work, and even from themselves. He was wrong about

---

[8]   Christian Smith, *Lost in Transition: The Dark Side of Emerging Adulthood* (Oxford University Press, 2011).

many things but not about that. Max Weber, writing in Germany about half a century later, argued that modernity would create an iron cage that would trap human beings within it—that the rationalization of society would eliminate mystery and humanity and the appreciation for that which is nonrational such as emotions, mystery, habits, and traditions. Weber predicted that the only thing that would set human beings free was the arrival of charismatic prophets or the discovery of ancient ideals.

Sociology and its prophets arose because the social world was changing rapidly, and the ground shifting under their feet. This shaking created space for sociological questions to emerge as the church and state lost their traditional authority. Similarly, I told my students today that this period of Covid-19 is the richest moment I have experienced in three decades as a sociologist. Why? Because there is room now to ask questions we would not have even have thought about asking a year ago. This is a time for creativity and imagination to emerge because the old ways of doing things are going out the window, and we get to create and imagine in ways we never even thought about before. In some ways, I told them, the pandemic has taken most of us out of our taken-for-granted realities and, as a result, has given us new eyes for seeing the world and discovering new things about it.

The same is precisely true for the church. God made it clear to Jeremiah that he was to do two things—tear down and build up, for that is the prophetic calling. Tear down those things that get in the way of God's highway to the new heaven and new earth and build up what is needed so that folks can access that highway.

The profile of Mennonite Church USA in 2006 revealed a church that was aging rapidly and losing its youth and young adults; a church that had become highly politicized since the early 1980s, a church that continued to struggle with racism both at individual levels and institutional and aggregate levels and so on.

As I wrote, these findings became the road signs for the project and the church. But as I looked at what was the dark side of the church, I remember the moment when I asked myself: "What if the Spirit is dismantling the church?" That was nearly 15 years ago, and from my perspective, what has occurred since then has only accelerated this dismantling—the scandal of abuse in Roman Catholicism, the embrace of Donald Trump and politics as the way to reform society by white evangelicals, the running away from the church of our youth, the fall from grace of evangelical leaders over issues of morality and integrity, and on and on. In so many ways, what we knew as the church is simply revealing ever more fully the dark side that we thought was sufficiently covered up. But the bones in the closet never lie, nor do they go away, and if we don't excavate them, we live under their power and deception forever.

In this way, the sociological perspective seems frightening to some, and is not, as Berger says, for those who prefer the "taken for granted reality" of what they learned in Sunday school or elementary school. But for those who are willing to take it on even for a brief spin—sociology has the power to show us the puppet strings by which we are being controlled and constrained. And that knowledge, says Berger, may be enough to set us on the path toward freedom.

In other words, both the prophet and the sociologist understand that we are always better off having our eyes open than closed—even when the news from the doctor is grim and tells us we have three weeks left to live. It is always better to live with open eyes, and that is the promise of both the prophet and the sociologist.

And so, if the Spirit is dismantling the church, I want to be among the first to help the Spirit. But when the Spirit turns to the building up, let me be there as well—for both are the work of the prophet and the work of the sociologist. And that is why I continue to teach sociology.

CHAPTER SEVENTEEN

When I Told God I Would Become a Pastor, and God Told Me When I Wouldn't

August 28, 2020

I'm so grateful that most of what the future holds is unknown to me most of the time. For if I knew what it was, I would do my level best to make sure it happens sooner rather than later or to make it disappear altogether, both of which are options that are more likely to create pain for me and those I love since my ability to make things work out in the end, has long proven faulty, unreliable, unpredictable. When Heidi, Jacob and I got back together after more than two years of separation, God graciously provided a much-needed job for me at Elizabethtown College teaching sociology. I loved it, and I still do.

But I still assumed that God would call me to some kind of formal ministry at some point or another since I had not become a missionary. Over and over, I repeated to Heidi and others that I would teach at the College until I turned 55. And then, I would go to seminary to become a pastor. I had it all figured out. In 1996, Heidi and Jacob and I began attending Elizabethtown Mennonite Church, where I was called to be an elder within a year or two. Within another year or so, the congregation needed a pastor, and a couple of folks sensed that I might be the one God was calling to lead the congregation. But I had a full-time job, and I wasn't sure how this would work out. But sure enough, the momentum to call me to the ministry continued. What was I to do about the College? I called my friend and Provost Ron McAllister and made an appointment to talk.

I explained to Ron the situation and he pressed me a bit on my sense of call. He was always a gentle soul with a rich depth of compassion. Once in a meeting with the Dean of Admissions, I had reacted pretty strongly about a situation that I felt deeply about. As I walked out of his office that day, Ron just looked at me and said, "You having a bad day? You could have been more magnanimous." And that was all Ron needed to say. I've never forgotten the moment.

I did have to look the word magnanimous up in the dictionary to figure out that Ron was telling me that I should have been larger and that I could have given more space and grace to others in the conversation. This has long been a challenge for me when I am anxious. But Ron's words were reprimand and rebuke wrapped in the grace and the benefit of a doubt that maybe it was just an "off day" for me. Oh, that I might be able to cover others' shortcomings in that same grace. I'll never forget that moment. I'll never forget Ron.

I left Ron's office, having told him what I sensed God's saying, and he told me later that he called the President, who replied, "Do we have to allow him to do this?" To which Ron—himself a devout Roman Catholic responded, "I don't think we have a choice. I believe Conrad has heard from God." And so, thanks to a college that has consistently supported and made space for my ministry of the past 20 years, a way was made to release me from a full-time teaching load in order to take on a pastoral call, a call that had come about 20 years sooner than I had scheduled it with God. Apparently God's administrative assistant had missed putting the date I had planned on heaven's calendar.

I was ordained in February 2000. I've often said those were the most difficult years of my life. Within two months I was diagnosed with papillary thyroid cancer and began a three-year journey of five hospitalizations, multiple surgeries, and radiation treatments. Later in that first year, I was asked by a prominent member of the congregation to resign, and who then distributed a letter to others in the congregation regarding this request. I would carry that pain for the remaining five years of our term.

In 2004 I was called to lead a study of Mennonite Church USA and decided I could not do everything on my plate. And so, we resigned from the ministry in August of 2005. I've often said it was God's grace to call me away from the congregation. But bless their hearts, they would call us back in 2011 and give us another chance. And so, since 2011, we've served in ministry at the same congregation. I believe it was God's grace that brought us back.

Then in February 2017, at the age of 52, I was diagnosed with Parkinson's disease. I am now the age at which I had anticipated going to seminary and moving into the ministry. I recognize, however, that there is no way I could be entering seminary and beginning a ministry call at this time in my life, given the Parkinson's disease diagnosis.

How grateful I am that God does not allow us to set our own schedules or develop our own plans and to create our own agendas. How grateful I am that I don't get to decide what happens and what doesn't happen in my life. The sooner we recognize this, the sooner we come to understand that any excavation work we are doing is being done in the context of the One who is the Grand Excavator. Any story we think we are writing is being written by the omniscient Author of all of history. The sooner we realize how weak we are, how poor we are, how broken we are, the sooner the Kingdom of Heaven becomes ours.

CHAPTER EIGHTEEN

About That Request for My Resignation and the Tragic Loss of Feet-washing to the Church

August 30, 2020

Within the first year of my ordination 20 years ago, a request was made by a prominent member of the congregation that I resign from my ministry role. The friend and brother who brought this request undoubtedly believed this was the appropriate response for a failure that I quickly acknowledged and confessed publicly to the congregation. My shortcoming was not unrelated to my struggle, mentioned in the previous chapter, to show magnanimity in situations where I have felt passionately and been anxious about a decision or issue, a struggle for which I continue to require the grace of Christ and the grace of others. The brother in Christ—who had called for my resignation—and I simply were not able to find a way to repair a relationship that I deeply valued, and I believe he did as well. And I'm sure the breakdown in the relationship was a disappointment to both of us. In any event, that cloud of my failure and his request hung heavy.

One Sunday morning, sometime after I'd announced that I would be resigning at the end of the five-year term, we celebrated Communion as a congregation and followed with the ritual of washing one another's feet. I grew up with this ritual. It was always a solemn affair—the men on one side of the church and the women on the other. It was a ritual based on the example of Jesus, who at the

Last Supper had washed His disciples' feet, a supper he was so eagerly looking forward to eating with them.

At Locust Grove Mennonite Church where I grew up, we would take off our shoes and socks and line up behind one another in the aisle. Walking to the front of the church, I would stand in line and watch young men and old men sit on the pew and stick their feet into a basin, sometimes with the lint from their socks clinging to their feet, feet that had walked many miles for their owners, and often very white feet, rarely seeing the light of day. Feet with lines from their socks, still impressed into those soft feet. Toenails deformed and toes going every which way except the direction they were created to go.

These feet were touched by the hands of another man who gently held them in those hands, and then sprinkled and poured water over those tired, worn, deformed old feet. Feet that had seen many a milking at 5 a.m., that had walked through many a field of alfalfa and corn, and feet that had also walked through pain and grief. Feet that walked down the aisle on wedding days. Calloused feet that had at one time been as soft and tender and plump as the beautiful little feet of our grandsons. Feet that we love to squeeze in our hands these days, for they're such small and tender feet.

But over time, something happens to our feet. Our feet begin to reflect the rest of us. Worn, tired, deformed, scarred, uncared for, calloused. I wonder what we could learn of ourselves and one another if we spent a little more time looking at our feet. But as churches, we've essentially given up this ancient ritual of washing one another's precious feet. It's gross. We say feet are stinky. It's no longer relevant. It was just a cultural thing in Jesus' day.

But interestingly, we don't say the same thing about Communion, even though we could. I mean, the whole idea of eating Jesus' body and drinking his blood is also pretty repulsive if you allow yourself to think about it. A lot more so than washing one another's feet. But we found a way to sanitize the whole Communion thing, taking away from it the power and mystery by reflecting on symbolism rather than the reality of that power and mystery. In taking away the eating of Christ's body and blood, we've taken away the sense of community and horizontal relationship. Doing away with feet-washing in the church has also meant that we've removed one more ritual that allowed us to come together as brothers and sisters in Christ and affirm our love for one another.

As a kid, after we had washed and gently and tenderly dried one another's feet, we would embrace the other man and give him some scripture and a holy kiss or something that affirmed who he was. Then we would go to the front table, put money in the alms offering as we called it (an extra offering that went to meet the needs of someone in our community), then back to the pew to put on our shoes and socks. Through all of this extended ritual, one man after another would spontaneously begin to lead a hymn, lifting their voices to words such as "Would you be free from your burden of sin; there's power in the blood," and "Amazing grace, how sweet the sound," and "Are you washed in the blood of the Lamb?" And those beautiful acapella male voices would blend together in a harmony that reflected the sacred power of the whole event. And above them all I would hear Dad's beautiful first tenor voice, reaching heights most of us could not, and always with that soft smile on his face that was sometimes less present at home.

There are so many good reasons we think it is time to be done with this irrelevant ritual. But there are so many good reasons that we are wrong once again as modern and postmodern folks. Leaving behind feet-washing has left behind one more way of being community together. One more way of finding healing and of acknowledging our brokenness. And one way to humbly offer our feet to one another to be cared for. I'm not sure I can imagine anything more beautiful than this way of gently and tangibly loving each other "just as we are" as grown men, hardened men, calloused men, men who rarely express emotions. Men taught to be strong men, taught not to reveal our weaknesses or to look in each others' eyes, and to acknowledge that we're all messed up. We're all as messed up as our feet. We're all the same in this moment at the foot of the cross. We all need Jesus.

And so, after four years of a painful relationship with a brother who asked me to resign, we had Communion and feet-washing. I went forward as usual and washed another's feet. When the two of us were finished, I looked up, and down the aisle came my friend with whom I had been unable to reconcile. He walked up to me and said, "Can we wash feet together?" "Of course," I said, and so we did. And I don't know that any words were spoken. At that moment no words were needed. I knew what he was saying to me and what we were saying to each other. It is over. We are forgiven, and we forgive.

When the congregation called Heidi and me to return to ministry six years after our resignation, one of my most significant concerns was whether or not my friend with whom I had washed feet would accept my return to leadership. And then I got a note from him asking me to breakfast. I was anxious, but my anxiety was unnecessary. As we ate, he looked up at me and said, "I want you to know that I will support you as you return to ministry once again." And true to his word, he always did so, regularly inviting me out for breakfasts that I began to look forward to because, in fact, we had so much in common. He offered me counsel, shared books he knew I would enjoy, and he and his wife made sure that Heidi and I had a steady flow of gift cards to our favorite coffee shop where he and I always hung out. My friend has since left our congregation. I miss those breakfasts. And like so many others I've lost track of, I miss my friend. Our times together were a rare, safe place for me with one of the last persons I ever thought I would feel safe with or who could accept me "just as I was."

So don't tell me God isn't in the restoration business. Don't tell me that the way the battlefield looks right now is the way it's going to look in the end. Don't tell me that there are times when relationships are over, where God is not continuing to work and to resurrect dry bones. And don't tell me again that feet-washing is irrelevant, meaningless, and has no place in today's sanitized version of the church, where we have rejected our humanity, where we have decided that the body is not part of who we are as human beings, where we believe that the only clean and manicured persons are those that belong. Because none of that is in the Bible.

CHAPTER NINETEEN

What Sociologists Are and What We Are Not—Keeping Our Eyes Wide Open, Knowing That Ignorance Is Not All It's Cracked Up to Be

October 4, 2020

There is no way I can teach a course in sociology anymore without mentioning Peter Berger, a longtime sociologist, now deceased. More than any other he has helped me understand society, my discipline, and myself. Berger has a way of writing, however, I tell my students, that occurred in a day when students actually read books. Or perhaps Berger just couldn't resist long sentences, long paragraphs, and long chapters, doing everything that good writers these days say we shouldn't do. Getting a bit rambling and lost in his pursuit of what he called the "doings of men."[9]

This week, my students read the first and last chapters of Berger's little book, *Invitation to Sociology.* He attempts to help the person on the street, the average person, the layperson, understand what sociologists do and who we are.

He begins by noting that there are no good jokes about sociologists, not because we fail to make idiots of ourselves; looking in those places we should keep our nose out of or speaking irreverently to people who yield big sticks. But because so few people on this planet even know we exist—it's hard to laugh about something

---

[9]   Peter Berger, *Invitation to Sociology* (New York: Anchor, 1963).

you don't remember and harder to joke about someone you've never heard of. Berger makes the point that the sociologist is not a social worker or psychologist, but more a philosopher or historian, one who is mainly interested in the question of what people are doing over there and why in the world they're doing it.

And the sociologist is not one who, when those questions start to percolate in their head, readily gives up and goes home and turns on the TV. No, the sociologist watches, observes, and listens. What are they saying? Who is saying it? How are they saying it? Who are they talking about? What will happen if they actually do what they say? Where are they going? The work of the sociologist comes down to investigative work driven by curiosity and a belief that things are not what they appear to be. The sociologist gets that, and in this Berger says is wisdom. But all of this gawking around at the world requires a few personal qualities that are not readily present in any of us. And particularly not among we who have such big egos in academia.

The first of these qualities is patience, patience to wait until something happens. Patience to listen to what is happening. Patience to test one hypothesis and then another and then another. For this is what science is really all about—nothing other than the debunking of one idea after another, rather like peeling back an onion, one layer at a time. A willingness to debunk what we assumed to be real and true and good, is the second value or quality of the sociologist, but once again something that most of us don't do readily. The sociologist lives for that moment when they can gleefully say to the folks in power, "I told you so. I knew none of you were wearing any clothes in that parade. I knew the emperor was as naked as a jaybird. What was wrong with you people that you believed him when you all knew that all along he was lying through his teeth?"

If someone were to come up to the sociologist and ask them, "How did you know the emperor had no clothes on?" they are likely to say something like this, "Besides the fact that my eyes told me so, I asked those little kids over there, and they told me the same thing." Because the sociologist bases their conclusions on empirical realities, on what our five senses tell us about what is true and real in the world, and not what I wish was really true in the world or not what I dream is real or true in the world.

And they depend not only on their own senses but also systematically ask what others see, often using surveys, focus groups, and interviews. But the sociologist knows that convincing folks that what they're looking at is a mirage or that what they're listening to is actually a lie or deception or malarky is not an easy task. As my friend and fellow sociologist Mike Schwartz likes to say, human beings have a kind of built-in rubber band that stretches for a time but usually pulls us back into what we've always believed to be real and true. In other words, it might be possible to convince a few folks that the king is naked. But sooner or later, even those who saw a naked king will begin to see him with his clothes on once again, not because he found his britches, but because they located their rose-colored eyeglasses through which they and everyone else look at the world.

In other words, the sociologist finds time and again that revealing the truth is usually an uphill battle, because most of society is so invested in burying the truth, even if it means they get buried in the process. This is why Berger asks rather whimsically whether we are harming undergraduates by feeding them the "poison" of a sociological perspective. He quickly says "not really," because students who spend a semester learning sociology and end up debunking much of what they learned in Sunday School or elementary school will, once the semester is over, be pulled by that rubber band back into position. And the truth they learned in a semester of undergrad sociology will go down the tubes. Instead, they will remember that cute boy or girl who worked with them on a class project.

In fact, Berger is so cynical about the interests of pursuing truth among undergrads that he claims they could care less what he does in class—whether or not he simply reads a phone book out loud. I often suggest to my students that if they could get their degree for the same price at Turkey Hill, which is a convenience store down the street, but without going to class, they would jump at the chance. And usually, nobody argues with me.

While Berger is cynical about the likelihood that a semester in the sea of sociology will cause the shipwreck of undergrads, he is much less pessimistic about the potential that lies within sociology for those who stick with it. The teaching and studying of sociology are justified, says Berger, among those who believe that it is "better to be conscious than unconscious and that consciousness is a condition of freedom."[10] In other words, sociology is a discipline that values living with our eyes open rather than closed. And sociologists believe that open eyes are more likely to lead us to freedom at the end of the day than are closed eyes.

I often tell my students at this point about my experience with cancer when I was 35 years old. I wanted to know the truth. "Doc, tell me the truth. How long do I have? Am I gonna make it? Is this treatment going to work? Is this surgery going to find what we need to find?" Three years ago, I was diagnosed with Parkinson's disease, and I still feel the same way. I want to know how many good years I've got. I want to know how long I'm likely to keep teaching. Tell me what my increased tremors mean this year.

And yet, there is more than just information or data that sociology offers us by encouraging us to live with our eyes open. In part

---

[10]   Invitation, 175.

because there is so much we as human beings don't know, including about diseases like the one I have.

What I really need to know is that I will be okay. I really need to know that my friends and family will walk this journey with me until that last and final breath. But if I keep my eyes closed to what lies ahead, I will also miss all the beauty of their company as I walk there. I will miss all of the beauty of creation that always looks brighter when we know we've got fewer days to live rather than more days. Keeping our eyes open touches the deepest parts of our hearts and causes us to make peace with whatever we see when they are open. But for those with their eyes closed, too often they are drinking or drugging themselves into oblivion.

I used to wonder what it must feel like to get old. I remember looking at my elderly grandfather, who I loved dearly, and wondering how in the world he lived with the knowledge that he would not live to see his grandchildren grow up or that at age 85, his days were seriously numbered. But at 56 years of age with Parkinson's disease, I am more than ever aware of my horizon. And especially when my family doctor says something like this, "Conrad, you have an all-encompassing disease, and you don't want that disease." As if I can close my eyes and make it all go away. Wishing it away will never heal me, and will only make me more miserable to live with.

But this diagnosis, because my eyes by God's grace are open as much as possible, has given me a view of the horizon of my life that I would never have gotten without this disease. And keeping my eyes on that horizon has caused not dread but joy. I now know what I want to do with my life and what I don't want to do. I'm not going to spend time on committees that do nothing. I'm not going to say yes to going out to lunch with people who just want to flatter me or who want to flatten me with criticism. Now I'm going to spend the days I have left with my dear wife and my best friend, with my son and daughter-in-law and grandsons, with my students who I enjoy so much, with traveling, and by enjoying the good gifts of a loving God. This disease and seeing the horizon have clarified my focus and what I really want to do with the rest of my life.

Keeping my eyes open to the diseases that I have and that are likely to contribute to my death will not make the conditions disappear. But keeping my eyes open will show me what I need to do to live the best life possible with the good days I have left. And for that reason, I would not close my eyes for the life of me, for the life of me is lived most importantly in its quality rather than its quantity.

So if you would rather live with your eyes closed, believing that ignorance is bliss, the table of sociology is not for you. But if you want to figure out the truth with others who want to live with their eyes open, sit down and join me.

CHAPTER TWENTY

A Love Letter to My Cancer
April 2000

I've faced my share of criticism for suggesting that the Almighty is behind the dismantling of the church—it's even been suggested by some that I am contributing to the dismantling. As a sociologist of religion, I am relieved by my knowledge that today's dismantling began decades ago in the United States. Like other sociologists, I am simply identifying the acceleration of trends that started even before my birth!

What seems to concern some folks, however, is my belief that God is somehow amid this dismantling, perhaps even responsible for it. But again, I am relieved by the knowledge that Scripture often identifies the Almighty with devastation, tragedy, and suffering. The Psalmist in chapter 46 blames God for the "desolations he has brought on the earth." It turns out, however, that the faith of the Psalmist causes him to see the devastation of God as good news, the good news of making "wars cease to the end of the earth..." and breaking the bow and shattering the spear, and burning "the shields with fire." The Psalmist recognizes that God ultimately turns disaster, devastation, and desolation into the ingredients that add up to Shalom.

I'm reminded of Michael J. Fox, who, in his most recent memoir about his Parkinson's diagnosis, describes his decision to return to acting despite his diagnosis, refers to having "co-opted" the disease to make it part of the family business. Fox found a way to cause

Parkinson's disease to work for him.[11] The question for we who claim Christ these days is, "Can we be still long enough to watch God co-opt the dismantling of the church and to turn it toward his Kingdom purposes?"

By claiming that God is behind the dismantling of the church, I am not abandoning hope. Instead, I am reclaiming it! But this has long been my view, formed during several periods of devastation and dismantling in my own life. The first was the nearly two and one-half year marital separation that Heidi and I experienced early in our marriage, a dismantling that God in his mercy redeemed and to which he indeed has brought shalom. But a second was my diagnosis of thyroid cancer at the age of 35, just after my ordination as Lead Pastor at Elizabethtown Mennonite Church.

This week, in cleaning out our attic, I found my journal from that period. And here is a loving word I wrote to that Cancer and which I shared with our congregation at that time:

> Two days ago, I learned that I have thyroid cancer. A journey has begun, not unlike the journey that started when Heidi and I separated now ten years ago. The journey of those years has become a significant point of reference, such that I often refer to the "before separation" and "after separation" moments of my life. I suspect that this experience will likewise divide my life into "before cancer" and "after cancer." For from now on, nothing will ever be quite the same. For years I believed that I was invincible, that nothing ever got me down. But now I have come to see that I am mortal. My life is fragile.
>
> But my first thought is to embrace you Cancer, talk to you as though you were a friend, but remind you that you must go, that you cannot stay within me. Your place in the natural world is a

---

11   Michael J. Fox, *No Time Like the Future* (New York: Flatiron Books, 2020).

product of sin. But you must be redeemed, and like all of nature, you must be washed in the blood of the Lamb. For all that is from sin and death must be washed, cleansed, and made whole.

So Cancer, my body is not the place to live and thrive. The place for you is in Jesus, the One who came to bear the effects of sin and to carry the sins of the world upon himself. You are not my enemy, Cancer, but a misplaced guest, looking for a home like all of us are looking for Home. You have found me, and for now, that residence seems safe to you. But we have discovered you, Cancer. We have found you out. You grew just a bit too much—just enough for Heidi to take notice of you. You thought you could hide, but your hiding place was found out like all products of sin and death. Light was shed on you. And now we bring against you all of the medical technologies available to us and the power of God to uproot you from your home. Like all sin, you became too greedy; your greed and self-ish desire became apparent.

But I'm not angry with you. I don't hate you. You remind me of that old cracked mug that I like so much because I so readily identify with it. For indeed I am broken, I am halved, I am cracked, I am partial. And your presence reminds me of these things, Cancer. And I needed that message. And your presence will be part of my biography forever. I will speak of the pre- and post-cancer days always.

But you do have to go Cancer. There is no room for you in this body of mine. Because if you stay, you will kill me, and if I die, you will too. You must go, you must be removed, you must be exorcised, and the blood of the Lamb must redeem you. I want to introduce you to the One who came to rid the world of sin and death. And in him, all of nature is being redeemed. You are only a part of nature. You are not sin, nor are you death itself. Instead, you are a product of sin, and you bring death. And so I pray for you, that you too will be redeemed, that being removed from me, you will find your rest in God, the One to whom I look for my rest and courage these days. Perhaps someday, Cancer, we will rejoice together as two who have found our lives and our futures in the Lamb of God who takes away the sins of the world. But for now, I ask you to leave me, to relieve me of the pain you will bring if you remain. I love you Cancer, and the Father loves you. If you allow him to lavish you with his love, you will never be the same. No one ever is who meets their Maker.

O Jesus, be with me. Care for me. Hold me. Let me cling to you as I've never clung to you. I have come to know you better; now may I come to love you more. O Jesus, have mercy on me. Have mercy on me. Have mercy on me. Have mercy on me, the cracked one.

And thus began what would become an intense three-year journey of multiple treatments and surgeries and nearly a lifetime of radiation. My prayer has continually been that the Father would keep the Cancer at bay, particularly during those early years of struggle and up and down prognoses. As it turns out, he has. For nearly 21 years, there has continued to be evidence of cancer in my body. Sometimes my annual bloodwork shows more and sometimes less. But for now, it has remained where it is.

It was good for me to reread this journal entry this week, and to remember that for decades I have believed the words of that old hymn I learned in chapel as a student at Wheaton College. That indeed, "every joy and trial falleth from above, placed upon our dial by the Son of Love. We can trust him fully all for us to do. Those who trust him wholly find him wholly true. Stayed upon Jehovah, hearts are fully blessed, finding as he promised, perfect peace and rest."

So be still my soul. And church, be still as well. Be still until you believe that all of this has come through God's hands. And as I tell dying saints, "his are the safest of all hands."

CHAPTER TWENTY-ONE

Grace Again, Tent Revivals Revisited, and Gratitude for Dad
April 24, 2021

O ver the past three decades, I have slowly but steadily moved toward the loving, outstretched arms of a God described by the Psalmist in chapter 103 this way: "As a father has compassion on his children, so God has compassion..." While this has been an ongoing, back and forth, and up and down journey, this past year of publicly dismantling my life through podcasting and writing has brought a more profound and more prescient experience of the grace behind God's compassion. As I unveiled, revealed, and confessed—I experienced a new awareness of God's acceptance of me "just as I am."

My experience of this past year, however, and of encountering the embrace of the God who holds me, much like that father in Rembrandt's awe-inspiring painting of the lost son come home, would never have occurred without my own dad's willingness, when I was in my 40s, to simply confess "I was never really a father to you, son."

At the time, now nearly two decades ago, I had been doing a lot of inner, personal work with a therapist to understand the pain and torment that I have experienced throughout my life—the deep inner shame, the condemnation that kept me up at night, the writing of confessions during exams when I should have been thinking of answers for the exam, and many other such efforts to gain peace in my heart. And so, as part of that personal work, I approached Dad on our screened porch and simply told him what it felt like to be his son at times—ashamed, abandoned, condemned, and unimportant. And without an ounce of defensiveness or self-righteousness or self-condemnation, Dad replied, "I'm sorry, son. I wasn't really ever a father to you. I didn't understand what you needed. I was too hard on you."

Among all of the healing words I've heard over almost six decades, these have been among the most important in my movement toward those loving and outstretched arms of God because, at that moment, I got a glimpse of those arms in the form of my father's immediate response of sorrow for his failures. At that moment, I became aware that my father could be trusted to accept me "just as I was" and to acknowledge the validity of my pain even if he hadn't understood it.

And over the years since that moment, my father, next to Heidi, my dear wife and loyal companion, has been my greatest advocate in moments when I have been unjustly accused by the saints, when I have been wounded for standing alone in moments when integrity was called for, and when I have needed counsel in complex situations. Dad has a way of speaking into my life these days that causes me to feel shielded and protected, such that even the criticism I've received for my writing and self-revelation over the past year has felt muted and less harmful than I would have experienced in the past.

Of all people who could have been most offended or unsettled by my vulnerability and openness this past year, it should have been my parents. They could readily have rejected, denied, or been embarrassed by my self-revelations. But several months after I had begun writing last year and being so open with my story and my song, we visited them. I wondered how they were taking and experiencing my sudden and public vulnerability. What I learned was that they were avid listeners, among my biggest fans, and Dad, with compassion in his voice, said, "Son, I've learned more about who you are over the last six months than I ever knew in the first eighteen years of your life."

And at that moment, I again felt those outstretched arms come around me just like those of the father in Rembrandt's painting. And I can now hear that father saying to his son words I'd not considered as part of that story before, "Son, I'm so grateful you have come home. I was not always a father to you, and I never really understood you. But one thing you never have to question again is whether my arms that embrace and protect you in this moment of your most significant brokenness, humiliation or vulnerability will ever fail to protect, defend, or advocate for you.

What I received from my father over the past two decades has helped heal the pain and torment I experienced in those tent revivals of George Brunk II. I am sure that George and others like him brought salvation to some, and I have no doubt he believed he was doing God's will. But what I never experienced in those moments, nor did I sense in the message or ethos of those meetings, was the compassion, kindness, acceptance, protection, and safety that I now find in my father from Big Valley and my Father in heaven, who over this year have "received me just as I am" and affirmed that "this is my story and this is my song," just as it is.

And so friends, "As a father or a mother has compassion, so God." And that is indeed divine grace and the Good News I had missed for so long.

CHAPTER TWENTY-TWO

The Good News About Sin That the Church Never Told Me
April 5, 2020

I grew up repeatedly hearing that the definition of sin was to "miss the mark." I knew that I was continuously guilty of sin because I frequently missed when throwing at God's dartboard. When I tried to clear the Almighty's high jump, I repeatedly fell short. My efforts to be good enough were never enough for a God who demanded perfection at everything.

The church told me that the good news was that Jesus came to deliver me from my sins and failures, but I never knew what to do with the fact that my sins and failures continued nonetheless and that since I hadn't reached perfection with Jesus, I must still be living in sin. And so I spent my life trying to be better, jump higher, throw more accurately—somehow proving to myself and those around me that I finally had achieved Jesus' approval by overcoming sin.

I wish someone had told me and all of us who were more than aware of our shortcomings that this was not Christ's definition of sin but of the Law from which Christ had come to set us free. The Law existed to remind us that we couldn't keep it—that was always God's intent in revealing the Law. The problem is that the church too often has become the keepers of the old rather than the heralds of the new, the trumpeters of damnation rather than the choristers of salvation. We have decided that the only way to keep our people and ourselves in line is to reestablish the Law, since God obviously could not have meant everything he said about grace. How would the church ever be the pure and spotless bride of Christ if we allowed folks to enjoy the freedom of grace for which Christ died? And the problem with living by the Law is that we are in a state of continual guilt, shame, and awareness of our failure—which keeps us tethered to a church that is afraid it might otherwise lose us. But losing its people at a faster rater than ever before, perhaps it is now also loosening its grip on the Law. We are Old Testament churches that teach about Jesus but don't receive Jesus. I am just beginning to understand how many have left the church because its preaching too rarely lives up to its promise. And some days, I feel full of grief and anger because of the lies of hell we've propagated and the truths of heaven we've hidden.

Here are just a few stories I've heard:

• One saint left the church because it taught that mental illness was sin—and this individual's family had a long history of depression and suicide.

• An older saint who lived all of their life under a burden of never being adequate only to recently tell me, with tears, that as a kid, upon sharing with his father that he had given his life to Jesus, heard his churchgoing father respond with, "Well, now you are really going to need to be good!"

• A church that recently asked me to speak, but in their publicity for the event noted that if we just "do church right then...".

Folks, I'm tired of this kind of teaching—teaching that denies our humanity, that holds a bar over our heads that God himself knows we can't achieve, and a belief that we can ever do church right.

This weekend a pastor who works with sex offenders emailed me and told me that he met with a group of men as he regularly does, and suggested they take Communion. One man refused, saying that he was too far from God. Then the pastor shared an essay about shame that I had recently written, and when he was finished, the man said, "Okay, I will take Communion now, and I am ready to try to walk with Jesus once again."

Last week, in my devotional reading, I came upon a more accurate definition of sin that is truly good news. It comes from the mystic Simone Weil. In it, she describes that Jesus went the furthest possible distance from God on the cross, a farther distance than any of us can ever go—separated from the Father because he was accursed as the Scripture declares. Weil says this: "[Those] struck down by affliction are at the foot of the cross, almost at the greatest possible distance from God. It must not be thought that sin is a greater distance. Sin is not a distance. It is a turning of our gaze in the wrong direction."[12]

Friends, we can never hit the mark of the law, but we can always turn our gaze back to Jesus. And when we do, we will always find him smiling at us, never rebuking us because we missed that damn mark again, never criticizing us for failing to jump high enough, but always saying, "Come back into my safe and loving arms, for today and every day hereafter, you shall be with me in paradise."

And that, my friends, is the truth of the Gospel that I choose to live with.

---

[12]   Simone Weil, *Love in the Void* (Waldon, NY: Plough Publishers, see https://www.plough.com/en/topics/faith/witness/love-in-the-void).

CHAPTER TWENTY-THREE

Memories of "Monger" and a Friend's Generous Reminder of That "Cloud of Witnesses"

June 1, 2021

Last week I received in the mail a small, about eight-inch, remarkably intact, rag doll with a small smudge on her face and long yarn braids. This gift had come unexpectedly from a Facebook friend who had also grown up in Big Valley but no longer resided there. She was aware of my ancestry and told me that she had received a rag doll 72 years ago from my dear great-grandmother, whom we all just called "Monger," apparently because one of her grandchildren had begun calling her by that name. And the name stuck.

Monger had grown up among the Nebraska Amish, who in the late 1800s moved by covered wagon from Big Valley, PA to the plains of the hot and dry midwest where they struggled through drought and fires and poverty, and for whom a cemetery remains to indicate that struggle. A thriving Russian Mennonite colony was just 70 miles further north, who had adapted by bringing wheat seed with them that could sustain the climate of the Plains. But the settlers from Big Valley had no such thing.

Monger was born in Nebraska and lived her formative years there until, at age 19, she and her family apparently admitted defeat and returned home to the valley. But for whatever reason, as a young woman, Monger never joined the Old Order Amish church and eventually became the homemaker for widower Joseph Renno. They would marry and have two sons—Erie and Paul. Erie was my grand-father, who I have spoken of in previous chapters as "Pap," overseer and dearly loved minister at Locust Grove Mennonite Church within the Conservative Mennonite Conference.

I was just seven when Monger died. She and I share the same birth date though separated by nearly 80 years. I remember Monger for her molasses cookies, sugar cookies, and sitting on her rocking chair braiding rugs. She was one of the saints, and I also remember her being part of the older women's "Amen" corner in our old wooden church structure. We sang hymns from "Life Songs" and the "Church and Sunday School Hymnal," always in acapella. Without accompaniment, the voices of the older women always rose above those of the rest of us and sounded as if they would break through the rafters into heaven itself.

This was especially true when we sang those beautiful old hymns about heaven that seem to have disappeared from our worship today. Their high voices were hauntingly beautiful, almost screeching at times, but a beautiful screeching from widows who were looking into heaven itself, and never more so when we sang "For God So Loved Us He Sent the Savior," first in English and then in German *"Gott is Dei Liebe."* And in those moments, all of us saw into heaven if we had any eyes with which to see such things. I will never forget when my mother got the call that Monger had been found dead, and the loud cry my mother made at that moment.

So when Alta Sharp Smith told me that she had a rag doll that Monger had given to her as a child at Locust Grove's sewing circle when Alta was just a little girl, I was thrilled to no end. And then, when she offered to give it to me, it felt like the kindness of God itself. Since receiving the doll whom Alta had called "Annie S. Renno" for seven decades, I have been reminded again of that cloud of witnesses of Hebrews 11 who cheer us on—those who have risked life and limb for their Lord and have known the horrific suffering of fires, drought, locusts and more on the plains of the Midwest. But these same folks continued to hold tight to their Savior and to keep their eyes focused on the Author and Perfecter of their faith, "who for the joy set before him endured the cross." For the joy. For the joy. For the joy that will come to the saints who make that long trek Home.

For some reason, one of my most vivid memories of Monger is her large, swollen legs, brown stocking covered and sticking out from beneath her long cape dress. Perhaps they were the first swollen legs of an aging person I had seen. Perhaps they appeared grotesque to a seven-year-old. But the older I get, and the longer I live with Parkinson's disease, the more I identify with those swollen legs, not because mine are swollen these days, but because those legs remind me of the journey that every saint makes. And though that journey often ends in a rocking chair with ghastly-looking legs—we all, like Monger, can continue to be of use to our Lord—baking sugar cookies, molasses cookies, braiding rugs, and deepening a life with God that only fixes our eyes more keenly on the joy yet to come and strengthens our understanding that our rocking chair and swollen legs are momentary, and nothing compared to the Glory just over that horizon ahead.

So when we pass on, though others may gasp and cry out when they get the news, we will already be screeching at the top of our lungs with the saints we've now joined in that glorious choir singing: "For God so loved us, he sent the Savior, For God so loved us and loves me too!"

Thank you, Alta, for sending Annie S. Renno to me at this season of my life to remind me again that Monger is in that cloud and has found that the Promises were indeed true!

CHAPTER TWENTY-FOUR

He Sang "Jesus Loves Me" and Was CPS Worker #008462

May 20, 2021

When we were kids growing up in Big Valley, we were blessed to have both extended families nearby. Many evenings were spent at my maternal grandparents—Erie and Verna (King) Renno— just "visiting." If it were summer, the cousins would play softball in the large lawn between the house and the chicken house, the latter being a way that Pap had found to subsidize his ministry income until it burned to the ground. Grandma always had candy—sometimes marshmallow peanuts or those little pink candies that taste like Pepto Bismol, but sugar is sugar when you are a kid.

We especially liked the ritual of visiting after church on Sunday evenings, begging to go to "Pap and Grandmas." But on special occasions such as Christmas or birthday gatherings, as we were all together, Pap would approach my cousin Ken Renno and me and ask if we would help him distribute the elements for a family Communion. Suddenly the loud noises and laughter that echoed through the basement quieted, and Pap would share with us how thankful he was for his family, what a privilege it was to see his children and grandchildren serving the Lord and moving on to take his place in the church as he got older.

What I see only now is that Pap was preparing his grandchildren for ministry. It was a ritual that also met a deep need that Pap had to feel the warmth of his family around him by enacting the

Lord's last evening with his disciples. I suspect our family Communion completed the gathering for Pap—it took an everyday event and made it a sacred one.

And then, invariably, he would ask us to sing, "Jesus loves me, this I know, for the Bible tells me so, little ones to him belong, they are weak, but he is strong." He often added that "you all know I can't sing," to which we grinned because we knew that already. And then we would sing.

I had no idea at the time what a blessing those family moments were. I understand much better now as a grandfather and father as we experience the gifts of adult children and grandchildren nearby. I don't know where Pap developed the longing to gather his children and grandchildren around him for Communion and to affirm Jesus' love. Still, part of me wonders if it wasn't the sacrifice he had made earlier in his life when unfairly drafted by the U.S. military. He answered that call by packing his bags, leaving behind a young wife and little ones, and heading off to CPS camp in Luray, Virginia—a camp for conscientious objectors administered by the Mennonite Central Committee in an arrangement with the federal government.

My mother, Ann, in her words, shares these memories of that experience for Pap and the family:

> Pap was drafted after he changed employers in Belleville. He never spoke with any bitterness about this but, I believe, saw it as God's hand leading him. The story he told included his being employed by a local dairy, Ka Vee Creamery, where he frequently needed to work on Sundays. Pap preferred to attend Locust Grove Church on Sunday along with his wife and two small children. In 1944, he was hired by the Belleville Flour Mills, which was not open on Sundays. The owner of the dairy, who also served on the local draft board, was quite unhappy about Pap's decision.

While Pap had a 2-year-old son and an infant daughter, and Grandma became pregnant with me, the draft board arranged for Pap to be drafted, which was against the regulations for drafting parents of multiple small children. Pap knew that this was the case when the creamery owner, who instigated his being drafted, actually came to him in later years and asked forgiveness. Pap's sharing about CPS experiences was always in light of his willingness to forgive another and to see the hand of a Sovereign God as the One who instigated the drafting.

I was born about four months before the official end of World War II, and Pap served in January 1946. Both Dad and Mother occasionally shared memories of that time apart for them. Dad shared that it was so hard to leave Mother and us children again on the few times he could come home! Mother, for her part, spoke very seldom about that time. Another local conscientious objector who was younger than Pap and unmarried at the time told a family member in later years of his going to pick up Pap to drive them both back to camp after a brief home visit, and how badly he always felt as Mother would be standing there with tears as Pap prepared to leave his young family.

Dad's memories included being asked to take on spiritual care responsibilities where he served at Luray, VA. I recall his sharing about these spiritual experiences more frequently than about the actual physical work he did. He always believed that God used those experiences to prepare him for the next phase of life. And, sure enough, after being honorably discharged from CPS, Pap was asked to be Sunday School superintendent at Locust Grove Mennonite Church. Then in 1951, the church asked him to consider being ordained as an associate pastor at Locust Grove.

Pap always saw God working in ways that proved he never wastes our experiences but always uses them again. I believe

Pap would say today that CPS during World War II was another way God was advancing His Kingdom in the hearts of men and women, boys and girls, and none of it was wasted.

As I look back on Pap's life, I long for more models of his kind of Christian faith in this divided time. For Pap was not divided—he was deeply committed to Jesus, understood that loving Jesus also meant he would forgive his enemies who betrayed him, saw the hand of a sovereign God in such a betrayal, and who chose to be a conscientious objector rather than take up the sword to defend religious freedom or anything else for that matter.

And I wonder, do we, the grandchildren, still remember that the Pap who sang "Jesus loves me" never separated his Christian piety from his Christian ethics—for Jesus was so clearly both his Savior and his Lord. I've thought of Pap a lot the last couple of weeks, and I know exactly what he would say in light of the fear, division, and chaos because he said it so often "Con, we just have to trust Jesus."

Amen Pap. Amen. And thank you.

CHAPTER TWENTY-FIVE

When Crisis Brings Conversion
June 11, 2020

I regularly tell my students that suffering is our best teacher—if we allow it to be. The most transformative moments of my life have been during the most profound crises of my life—the more than two years that Heidi and I were separated, two separate bouts with cancer—both thyroid in 2000 and salivary gland in 2014, Heidi's experience with ovarian cancer, my diagnosis of Parkinson's disease, and several church crises that some days I thought would take me under.

With the list of crises I've just noted, sometimes I think I must be a very hard-headed saint. I regularly pray and have done so for years, "Lord, do in my life whatever it is that you want to do to make me who you created me to be." And yet, every one of these crises has been a moment of conversion for me, a moment when I was "forced" perhaps to go deeper in my life with God because, as I so often say, "What alternative do we have?" We either go deeper with God or choose death, which always comes when we abandon God because we abandon the only Life there when we leave God.

And perhaps that is what the old tent revivals with George Brunk II and others were an effort to do—to bring us to a crisis in our lives and to push us to decide between life and death. And while this message may have been compelling for some, the problem for me as a kid was that I was already aware of the crisis I was in and didn't need to be reminded by others. What I needed amid my torment, doubts, fears, and insecurities was the experience of a God who was waiting to save me, of a God who did accept me "Just as I am," of a God who was running toward me, of a God who offered me hope every morning when I awoke. But that God remained in the dark.

Getting to a point in my life where I am more aware than ever of this loving God, has required crises, those moments when the world that I took for granted to be the true, real and best world was cracked open by some divine earthquake. Everything I took for granted was up for grabs: Would our marriage ever be restored? At 35 years of age and diagnosed with cancer, would I live to see our little boy grow up? Would Heidi live beyond five years with a cancer that is often a death sentence? Would I survive one more church conflict? And now, what will my end be like with Parkinson's disease, and where I am on this journey? How long will my health hold out? Will I end up with dementia? And on and on. For it is in the moments when life's answers are most out of reach that some of us finally reach for God.

Coming to know God has required being in a place of needing God. To come to know God, I have had to be in crises where the questions overwhelmed any easy answers that so many saints wanted to offer. To come to know God, I had to walk with God into and through the pain and uncertainty. As did Job of the Old Testament, and as we all do well to understand, I had to learn that there are few readily available answers as to why bad things happen, and knowing would be unlikely to give us peace anyway. What brings peace is knowing not the answers but the One who has them even if he won't share them with us when we most think we need them. Knowing God and knowing all of the answers that I think I need are two very different things. We will worship one or the other, but we can't honor both at the same time.

I've long loved a prayer by Peter Marshall, former chaplain to the U.S. Senate who thanked God for every need that kept him close to Christ's side. And I think I've needed every one of these crises after all. But I am not alone. Not only is suffering our best teacher but it might also (with God in the midst of it) be our only teacher.

The history of God's people is precisely this. In my reading this morning in Psalm 78, the writer reflects on the lengthy history of this pattern where time and again, in response to the people's complaints, God answered with water, food, deliverance, protection. And yet, his response was rarely sufficient as they continued to complain. And so God disciplined them, sometimes quite harshly from our perspective.

But the discipline of God is always more about restoration and redemption than it is about retribution, as the Psalmist notes: "Yet he was merciful; he forgave their iniquities and did not destroy them. Time after time, he restrained his anger...He remembered that they were but flesh, a passing breeze that does not return."

Throughout all of Scripture, the crises we walk through are always within the context of a loving God who loves us too much to allow us to remain just as we are. While he always receives me "Just as I am," when I surrender to him (the secret ingredient of all the saints), he begins to chisel away at the residue of darkness and death that has accumulated throughout my life. And while the chiseling is uncomfortable and even painful some days, it always emerges from the heart of One who knows what I've covered up and the beauty that his chiseling will reveal.

CHAPTER TWENTY-SIX

Recovering From Those Tent Revivals
by Remembering Pap's Grace
April 20, 2021

It's become clear over the past year that I am in recovery mode. A member perhaps of TRA or Tent Revivals Anonymous—"Yes, I'm Conrad, and I walked that sawdust trail more times than I can count." Jesus must have been so confused by how many times I asked him to come into my heart. I suspect he was more sad than confused—sorrowful that I felt a need to invite him into a soul within which he already lived and to which he had already brought hope and life that I was so unable to hear over the din of George Brunk's preaching and the sound of those around me singing "Just as I am." I couldn't figure out why most of them felt that being just as they were was just okay with Jesus, but just as I was, well, wasn't.

I've also shared about the oppressive "Old Order" culture that demanded conformity in a valley where most of us who were Mennonite had emerged from that Old Order gene pool. Though escapees from technological and dress restrictions, we remained captive to a religious tradition that by and large, as expressed in Big Valley, was relentless in sorting out the wheat from the chaff and the sheep from the goats. Within that pressure cooker, one either pretended to be wheat and sheep and got used to the deception or acknowledged that you were chaff and a goat and thus went forward at every altar call you could.

I know I see things through my own subjective lens and I am sure that others experienced this culture differently than I did. I've also heard from enough folks who have left the valley or remain there yet, to know that Tent Revivals Anonymous could be a legitimate support group if the effort was made to organize it.

But my grandfather "Pap," for whatever reason, was an anomaly in the valley. Knowing what I do now, he was far ahead of the Lancaster Mennonite Conference Bishops of his time even though we in the valley all assumed that Lancaster folks were far ahead of us in just about every other way. Pap did away with the "common" Communion cup long before his peers in Lancaster. Pap abandoned Council meetings before Communion—in which one either had to publicly shame oneself by acknowledging that they were not at peace with God or their neighbor. The alternative to being shamed was to lie through your teeth and say, "Well, of course, I am." The fact is, only in heaven is that a truthful answer if the truth be told.

Pap also accepted back graciously into the church those who had chosen to fight the war in Vietnam. Before his death, Pap encouraged one of his granddaughters to pursue formal ministry despite the fact that his own Conservative Mennonite Conference of Rosedale, Ohio, still does not endorse women's leadership gifts. And to his dying day, he regretted a decision he had made to invoke harsh discipline upon a woman who had experienced a divorce.

Pap hung out at the Belleville Restaurant even after it scandalously began selling alcohol. Pap was known for his love for others more than his judgment, for his grace more than his condemnation.

It's been a puzzle to me why I so allowed George Brunk II and his tractor and trailer contraption, to be such a prominent and brooding figure in my little kid life. And why my Pap, who loved Jesus as much as anyone I've ever known, and who insisted that we sing "Jesus loves me, this I know" at every family gathering, for so long remained the minor chord in my spiritual memory. Indeed, I don't remember a condemning sermon by Pap nor even an altar call of his that I responded to. In fact, I don't remember Pap offering an altar call at all.

Rather than fighting the fears of a dismantling church, being threatened on all sides by the changes of modernity, by demanding conformity and declaring us all on our way to hell unless we lived right, dressed right, smelled right—you get the point—Pap offered Jesus, a kind Jesus, a loving Jesus, a gracious Jesus, a sweet-smelling Jesus.

I know that some and perhaps many assume I've gone soft on sin over the last year and have become lukewarm rather than hot and lost my first love. But I beg to differ. What I've rediscovered is the piety and deep love for Jesus of a grandfather whose experience of that deep, broad, high, and lengthy love mirrored that of St. Paul the older he got.

I am facing a horizon that I am much more aware of today than ever before. And as that horizon approaches, the hell-fire and brimstone preaching of George Brunk II and the condemning conformity of my home community are simply receding in the light of the future glory that is coming into clearer view for me now. And my goal, now more than ever, is to join the Spirit of God in excavating that Isaiah 40 highway so that as many as possible can come to experience the same love of that Spirit as I have over this past year.

Though my detractors may disagree, I do not doubt that I have both experienced the love of Jesus and had as much of a Pentecost experience as I've ever known since my diagnosis of Parkinson's disease. And though you may disagree with me, I know more than ever and am more boldly than ever singing wherever I go, "Yes, Jesus loves me, Yes, Jesus loves me."

And whatever you happen to be recovering from, Jesus loves you, too.

CHAPTER TWENTY-SEVEN

Why Jesus Loves Those Who Are Blind and Turns a Blind Eye to Those Who See

October 18, 2020

A redeemer corrects a past failure, mistake, or sin of another. Jesus understood that his mission was to save those who were victims of failure, sin, mistakes—of their own doing or the doings of others. In Luke 4, as he begins his ministry, he quotes the prophet Isaiah: "The Spirit of the Lord is upon me because he has anointed me to preach good news to the poor, He has sent me to proclaim freedom for the prisoners, and recovery of sight for the blind, to release the oppressed, to proclaim the year of the Lord's favor." (Luke 4:18)

What Jesus is saying to the poor, to the powerless, to the blind, to the oppressed, to the prisoner is, "Hang in their child—your day of redemption has come. If the wealthy, the powerful, those who can see, and the oppressors aren't going to redeem you—I am!" But at the same time, he was clearly saying to the wealthy, the powerful, those with sight, and the oppressors—"Your day of reckoning has come. What you would not do, I will do. What you failed to correct, I will now redeem."

This is the excellent news of the Gospel friends. This is why the Gospel is such good news to those who are most down and out—because the Gospel promises to correct the wrongs that were done to you—the abuse, the ridicule, the laughter, the gossip, the trauma, the curses, the judgment.

Yes, Jesus is the Redeemer, but only for those who need to be redeemed. Only those who are blind. To everyone else, he turns a blind eye. Jesus had a thing for blind people—he saw them in the crowd, he responded to their cries, he heard the injustice they experienced. And he redeemed them. In the Gospel of John chapter 9, John tells us that Jesus and his disciples were walking along one day, and Jesus sees a man who has been blind from birth. The disciples are immediately intrigued about the sin, mistake, or wrong that this man or his parents had committed, leading to this lifelong blindness. So who sinned here, Jesus?

But right away, we see the difference between one who is a redeemer and those who are not. Those who are not redeemers move right in for the kill—who sinned Jesus so that this guy has had to suffer? I mean, someone must have screwed up. Give us the juicy details, Jesus, you who know all things. Who was it, and what did they do? Maybe we can get it published in the *National Enquirer!*

But the Redeemer was quick to respond—nobody sinned—neither his parents nor this man. And then Jesus does what only a Redeemer can do; Jesus takes the man from the judgment of his disciples and elevates him to a work of God. Jesus takes the defective one and makes him the honored one. Jesus takes the one that others rejected for his imperfections and places him into God's story. A man of no account is suddenly given a God story. A man with a bad story is suddenly placed in the best story ever. A man who was rejected by the disciples is now accepted in God's story.

"Neither this man nor his parents sinned, said Jesus, but this happened so that the work of God might be displayed in his life." Do you hear this? The young man was blind from birth so that the work of God, which is always a redemptive work if we allow it to be, could be done in his life. I think of Paul's words, "You are God's workmanship" or "God's handiwork." (Ephesians 2:12)

When we think of God's workmanship or that we are God's artwork or handiwork—we tend to think of perfection and that which is beautiful and lovely—but not that which is defective or unlovely or unattractive or repulsive. That's because we don't look at others the way a redeemer does. The redeemer says—I am here to correct past wrongs. I am here to restore the work of God. I am here to make whole. But a redeemer can only work with those who know they need to be redeemed. Jesus said this over and over. I came for the one sinner, not the ninety-nine in no need of repentance; I came for the sick and not the healthy who don't need a doctor. The degree to which God can do his work in us is directly related to how willing we are to acknowledge that we are defective, blind, imperfect, and broken. Jesus walks around looking for blind folks who want to be healed—everyone else he is walking right by.

And so, Jesus healed the man, and at this part of the story, Jesus disappears from view. After such incredible act of redemption has just occurred—why would the man still need Jesus? After all, everyone will be celebrating! A blind man can see! His parents, the Pharisees—why everyone will surely be delighted that this man has been redeemed! Why, of course, that's how the story will go. But of course, it does not.

It turns tragically against the one who has been healed—for too many of us just don't want the blind to see; the prisoners to go free; the lame to walk; the poor to sit at the table with us. And we certainly don't want to hear their stories. Like the disciples, we have some investment in walking around and looking down our noses at all those poor folks who don't see as we do, who just don't have quite the godly perspective that we have. As long as they remain blind, our theology of God's judgment and our righteousness can stay pretty much intact.

The wonderful thing about Jesus—is that when he looks at a blind man or blind woman—he could care less about our theology or righteousness or whether someone should be healed on the Sabbath or not—what Jesus sees is the work of God that is about to be revealed in that man or woman's life; what Jesus sees is a redemption project. He doesn't care what the rest of us see or don't see.

And so, as the story goes on, those who had known the man when he was blind get all tangled up in the question of whether this is indeed the man who was blind. And if so, how did it happen? Where is the man who did this?

At this point, the one who has been redeemed and his eyes restored finds his voice and creates a story of his experience that he will keep repeating. How sad this man must have felt. Instead of celebrating with him, his friends and neighbors challenge his story and his experience of redemption.

Sometimes we experience good news that we can't wait to share with others, but as we begin to share our story—we find they are dismayed; they don't like our story; they never knew we had this story before; they don't believe what we are seeing; they liked us better when we were blind and quiet. No, we don't always appreciate when those around us begin to tell their story of being redeemed by Jesus. Perhaps we feel threatened because we don't have a redemption story of our own. And so for the blind man and for many of those touched by Jesus, the controversy only grows.

These neighbors who don't like the story they hear the blind man singing—which is simply the testimony of his experience with Jesus—now take it to the religious leaders, the Pharisees, so that they can investigate the story.

Folks, think with me about the ridiculousness of what is happening here, except that tragically it isn't that far away from the reality of what the blind still experience when they are given their sight.

The Pharisees only complicate things by accusing Jesus of healing on the Sabbath. When asked, the formerly blind man tells his story again: "He put mud on my eyes, and I washed, and now I see." Friends, the redemption story is so simple. Hearts are cleansed. Eyes are opened. Broken limbs are healed. Sins are forgiven. Wrongs are corrected. But it only happens to those who know their hearts are broken, who know they can't see, who know they are lost, and who know they need a redeemer. And when it happens, and if it has ever happened to you, you know there will be a backlash, often among those from whom you least expect it. And it's always among those who think they can see.

So the story moves from Pharisees to the man's parents, who are now brought in for questioning. Can you imagine as parents? You have prayed with these same leaders, perhaps for your son to be healed, but the moment he is, they turn on you. "We don't know," they said as they turned their backs on their son, "Ask him. He is of age. He will speak for himself."

This young man must have felt like his last potential allies in the world had just abandoned him. Given a chance to courageously stand with their son in the best moment of his life and the one they had prayed for years to see, they gave in to fear and cowardice. Do you see that the only one with courage in this story is the one who is now standing accused, the one who was healed? But then he was probably used to that. When he was blind, he was harrassed, and now that he can see, he is accused. And yet, he was so courageous.

Although this experience must have been upsetting, confusing, and painful for this young man, his courage in the face of his accusers is evidence that he had indeed met Jesus, that the work of God was being done in his life even as he faced them. Because when the work of God is being done in our lives, we are always becoming more authentic human beings, authentically who God created us to be. When God's work is being done in our lives, we are always in a place of significant vulnerability in which we are exposed to the rejection of others, but we are also finally becoming authentic. I wonder if the fact that Jesus walked away from the young man following his healing was perhaps Jesus' way of testing just how deep the transformation of this man's sight had gone. Had it gone deep into his soul? Had he now come to believe and to see that he was indeed a work of God and one in whom God was at work no matter what anyone else said?

We observe his courage just grow and grow. He moves from simply telling his experience of healing to getting right in the face of his accusers. Listen to his response to the Pharisees: "Whether he [Jesus] is a sinner or not, I don't know. One thing I know, I was blind, and now I see!" And then this: "I have told you already, and you did not listen. Why do you want to hear it again? Do you want to become his disciples too?" And then this after they declared themselves disciples of Moses but that they didn't have any idea where Jesus came from, the young man responded: "Now that is remarkable! You don't know where he comes from, yet he opened my eyes. We know that God does not listen to sinners. He listens to the godly man who does his will. Nobody has ever heard of opening the eyes of a man born blind. If this man is not from God, he could do nothing."

This was all too much for Pharisees who did three things that those who are threatened by a story of God's restoration and healing are tempted to do: They went back to their old argument that he was "Steeped in sin at birth." They wielded their authority by asking, "How dare you lecture us? And they threw him out.

What a tragic, tragic story. A blind man is healed, a prodigal comes home, a prisoner is set free, a slave escapes—but rather than celebrate, they accuse, condemn, and reject. They do everything they can do to shut down his testimony.

But all the while, unbeknownst to the young man, Jesus has been watching him; Jesus is aware of the condemnation, the pain, and the rejection. And as Jesus always does to those he has redeemed but others have rejected, he comes to the young man.

Those of us who have been redeemed by Jesus and set free by his Spirit, and who in trying to tell our story, only to find that it is rejected, judged, and condemned—can always count on Jesus showing up. One of the benefits of being judged and condemned by everyone else is that we finally see that no one is safe except Jesus; and that there is no safe place except with Jesus. The best thing that could have happened to this young man was perhaps his rejection by others so that when Jesus showed up, he was so ready to worship Jesus, prepared to give his life to Jesus, set to hang out with Jesus.

I wonder if the rejection, judgment, and condemnation of this young man wasn't just part of the work of God that Jesus promised as a reason for his blindness from birth. Because when we are freed from our fear of what others say about us or what they think of our stories of Jesus—there is no stopping us, no way no how! The real freedom and the most significant work of God in this story is not the deliverance from blindness but rather deliverance from thinking that anyone besides Jesus could be his redeemer, defender, and refuge.

There is no other place of rest. There is no other place of safety. There is no other place of security. I am at a place in my life where I enjoy my time in the morning, sitting safely in God's presence, listening to music, meditating on a psalm, lifting people and situations to God, and just feeling more secure and accepted there than anywhere else I will be the rest of the day. There is no shame in that place anymore, no condemnation, no judgment, no accusation.

And when we arrive at that place we come to understand that God is enough. That God is all we need. That with God, we are always safe. And in comparison, both the flattery of others or their accusations, judgment, and condemnation have less hold on us anymore.

But the story of the blind man who can now see doesn't end yet, for Jesus goes on to clarify that he does bring judgment—a judgment that will allow the blind to see, but those who see to become blind. The Pharisees perked up at this. "You talking about us," they muttered, about to get all bent out of shape again. Jesus responded: "If you were blind, you would not be guilty of sin, but now that you claim you can see, your guilt remains."

If we are to come to experience Jesus as our only safe place, our only rest—then we will all have to admit that we cannot see. Doing so will release freedom and deliverance and joy and courage and authenticity. It will also remove condemnation and judgment, and criticism from others. But that will only remind us that our rest is in God alone and drive us invariably, if we allow it to do so, into his loving arms.

CHAPTER TWENTY-EIGHT

An Unexpected Addendum to the Last Chapter About the Blind Man
October 20, 2020

I keep thinking about that blind man from the previous chapter and how unusual it is for us to stick to our story of freedom in the face of ongoing resistance and pressure from others. I can imagine the young man eventually getting to the point of saying something like, "Well, maybe my neighbors are right—maybe I can't see after all…things do seem to be a little blurry after all…maybe this whole healing thing is my imagination at work rooted in my desire to see… maybe I was the victim of a snake oil salesman after all and not a prophet of God…if that is the case, perhaps my sight was a curse, and I was better off being blind…" and on and on. Because in the face of resistance, ridicule, and unbelief, so much of the time, we choose to believe what others say about us rather than the redemptive story that we know has happened in our lives.

Choosing a false narrative of others rather than the authentic story of redemption and the Spirit's work that we know is ours will always lead to despair, resentment, depression, etc. The closer we come to Jesus, the more we become our authentic selves—the one God created us to be. The closer we draw to Jesus, the more we lose the false self and gain the true self, created in God's image. But the more we resist Jesus, the more we hang out in that space where we try so hard to conform to what everyone else wants us to be, assumes that we are, remembers us to be, prefers us to be, and on and on. It is terrifying to leave that space of belonging because so often, those we thought loved and cared for us will no longer journey with us.

The young man whom Jesus healed chose to stick with the story that was right and just and true, and at least for the moment, seems to have lost all of his relationships. But in the end, he gained Jesus. And in the end, only Jesus will matter.

When we stand before Jesus, none of our family will be there with us. None of our friends. None of our neighbors. Not our spouse or our children. It will just be God and me having the most honest conversation we've ever had. But the good news is that we can begin that conversation here and now—which when we do so makes it not something so much to dread but something so much to look forward to. For though I see through that darkened glass for now—we will someday see Christ face to face—and when we do, we will also finally see ourselves as God saw us all along, and we will finally know how deeply we were loved.

Over the years, I have learned that my mother gets relatively little sleep at night. She is often up praying and reading the Scripture. Her love for God's word and her sense of what God is saying as she prays have been a comfort and guide for us over the years and a legacy I hope to pass on to those who follow me.

When I was diagnosed with Parkinson's disease in 2017, she sensed God leading her to John 9, the story of the blind man about which I shared in the last chapter. In particular, Mom felt led to point out to me Jesus' words that this man had been born blind so that the work of God could be revealed in his life. I have found great comfort in that word from Mom and the promise that no matter what might be happening to me from the perspective of my health, the work of God is being displayed in my life in a way that would not have been possible without this disease. Perhaps it was in having this disease that Jesus would open my eyes and give me sight that

I never had before. Perhaps in his coming to me, he set me free as one can only be set free when delivered from the opinions, criticism, condemnation, and judgment of others. Perhaps our sight depends on such freedom, and perhaps our liberty depends upon such sight.

Given my mother's word, I see this story of the blind man differently than I ever have before—that through my diagnosis of Parkinson's disease, the work that God has been up to within me has not been about healing me physically but rather freeing me from the terror and pain and fear of God's wrath within which I had lived for decades. And along with that, freeing me from the fear of what others would say about my story and song.

As I look at the uncertain horizon of my life, I am no longer willing to be dishonest about what is within me. And if that means I lose friends I thought were friends—I would rather that than lose my soul. I still get worried about what other people think, given all I have shared across the different worlds I live and engage within. I feel pretty vulnerable some days. But I am more free and at rest these days than ever before, and I also live more consistently within my identity as a child of God.

That freedom and identity have been reinforced by one of the greatest gifts I have received since I began writing eighteen months ago, and that has been my parents' affirmation of what I have been sharing, and my dear father's appreciation that he has gotten to know me so much better than he ever knew me before—that he has learned more about me in five months than he ever knew me while I was growing up.

How Dad's appreciation for what I've written warmed me at the moment he shared this with me, for if Dad is the only one who appreciates my story and understands me now more fully—that has made the entire year of writing worthwhile. When you are honest and vulnerable and still loved by those closest to you, it doesn't matter what anyone else says about your newfound freedom. What I knew then and know still is that the acceptance and embrace I experienced from Dad is like that which our Heavenly Father is just hanging around waiting to give each one of us—Jesus' story of the prodigal son and of the blind man made whole could not make that truth more clear.

CHAPTER TWENTY-NINE

An Unexpected Addendum to the Last Unexpected Addendum About That Blind Man

October 21, 2020

In my introductory course in sociology, I always show at least part of the movie "The Truman Show." This film with Jim Carey is timeless in its depiction of how most human beings live most of the time. Truman is born on a movie set in a town created just for him along with the actors who support the ongoing production of what to everyone else is a movie but to Truman is the real world of his life.

As he grows up, Truman has no idea that he is on a movie set or that those around him are acting out their roles and then going home at night and collecting a paycheck for their acting. To Truman, this is just his world—the real and true and right world. Until things begin to happen, like a stage light falling from the sky in front of him, ongoing barriers to his leaving the island on which he lives, like the return of his father whom everyone had always said was dead, and on and on.

Slowly it begins to dawn on Truman that maybe his "taken for granted reality" is not actually all that real or true or right and that perhaps he's been deceived all along. He is encouraged in questioning his world by a young woman who intentionally wears a pin that asks, "How will it end?"

It turns out that how it will end is up to Truman, who finally risks his life trying to leave the island by boat despite his fears of the water and despite the best efforts of the director to destroy the boat and Truman with an artificially created storm at sea. Kristoff, the director of the show about Truman, had much invested in Truman being content with the false story of his life just as many in our lives have the same investment. But Truman does survive, and breaks through the island wall. The film ends with the anticipation that he will be reunited with Meryl.

In many ways, Truman's story reflects that of the blind man in John 9 who, when healed, refused to accept the narrative that those around him had constructed for him. Against all of the resistance of others, he insisted on sticking with his story—"I can see. I have been healed. I don't know who did it, and I don't care what any of you think."

This is so hard for most of us to do. We spend our energy trying to conform to the expectations of those around us—to do what they want, live as they want, say what they want—even when the cost is the shrinking of our souls. We so often quote Jesus's words about losing our souls but gaining the world. Still, I'm not sure that we understand the fullness of what Jesus might have meant—I think it might be as simple as the choice we have to conform to what everyone else expects of us and what the culture around us says is right and proper and good and lose who we are and who God created us to be in the meantime.

So often we are like rubber bands that for a moment, allow ourselves to be pulled to consider possibilities other than those which we and others take for granted. Still, most of the time, we will enable ourselves to pull back to what we always assumed was proper and reasonable because the tension from believing anything else just becomes too great for us. Rather than live in that tension, we surrender to the pressures, and when do so, we lose those most creative and mysterious moments that crises offer us to learn about ourselves, others, and of course, God.

I often challenge my students to live with their eyes wide open to the world around them, even when it brings anxiety, fear, or uncertainty. As I shared in a previous chapter, ignorance is not the bliss it is so often cracked up to be. When we close our eyes to what we fear, we also close our eyes to the hope that overcomes our fears. Had the blind man accepted the taken for granted reality that people tried to assign to him, had he decided that everyone else was right and that his story of Jesus' healing him was fiction—I don't think he would have had his eyes open to see Jesus when Jesus shows up at the end of the story either.

So often, I hear folks say—"I don't hear God speak to me, or I've never seen God do anything." I suspect the problem is less God than the likelihood that those same individuals have missed seeing and hearing an awful lot of other things in the world around them. For when we open our eyes to see the world as it truly is and not as everyone necessarily says that it is—we will see what is real and true and good—and there is none more real, more true, or more good than the One who opened the blind man's eyes.

CHAPTER THIRTY

If You Pray the Sinner's Prayer, Squeeze My Hand
December 17, 2020

My father-in-law's reputation had preceded him. A sinner, of course, his was one of those doors I had knocked on as a kid when our church group went door to door with those little tracts called "The Four Spiritual Laws." That's a pathetic title, for such good news of grace that in fact did away with such spiritual laws.

Upon marrying his beautiful and grace-filled daughter, I understood that my father-in-law carried enough pain that try to or not, it couldn't help but spill out upon everyone around him. But upon our marriage separation that occurred just three years after our wedding, and when our son Jacob was 18 months old, we would visit Kerry so that he could spend time with Jacob. In those years we spent more time together than ever before. And in those moments of bonding, a relationship began to grow between the two of us. I experienced a soft heart I hadn't seen before, a generous heart hidden beneath deep wounds. I began to value our relationship. And there were times when Kerry allowed me to pray with him.

But at the age of 49, he suddenly experienced a brain aneurysm that became serious quite quickly, and he was soon a patient in critical care in a large medical facility. In one of the moments as we sat in the waiting room, Heidi asked if I would talk with her dad about the condition of his soul and his readiness to meet Jesus. So I went back to Kerry's room, where he was nearly beyond recognition with the tubes and wires around him and his head wrapped so tightly in bandages. "Kerry," I said, taking his hand. "Do you know where you are?" "The hospital," he quietly spoke.

"Yes, you're in bad shape, and we're not sure you're ready to meet God. I'm going to pray with you to give your life to Jesus. And if you pray this prayer with me when I have finished, just squeeze my hand." I began to pray for Kerry to receive Jesus and be forgiven for all of the sin, shame, blame, and pain he carried.

For our sin—our choosing to live in the dark—is the one thing that keeps us from God, but fortunately not God from us. George MacDonald, that Scottish poet of the 19th century whom C. S. Lewis credits for influencing his own life, has written a sinner's prayer that I so appreciate: "Oh Christ my life, possess me utterly, and make a little Christ of me. If I am anything but thy father's son, Tis something not yet from the darkness won. O give me light to live with open eyes, Oh give me life to hope above all skies."[13]

Too often, we have made the sinner's prayer one of condemnation and shame. But of course, we would feel a need to do so if the message we are told is about our failure to keep the four spiritual laws. But what if we started instead with grace, with good news, with news that God so loved the world and loves it still? What if we began to call it the "saint's prayer" of homecoming and restoration and grace?

This coming to Jesus and the prayer that accompanies it need not be complicated. It certainly wasn't for the thief on the cross. He simply turned his face to Jesus, saying, "Remember me." And remember Jesus did and still does. Even when that prayer is breathed in silence on one's deathbed and the amen to that prayer is a tightly squeezed hand. For no sooner had I finished praying than my father-

---

[13]   See https://books.google.com/books?id=kGVODwAAQBAJ&dq=macdonald+o+give+me+life&source=gbs_navlinks_s.

in-law gripped my hand so tightly as if to leave no doubt that he had prayed with me.

And in that moment, to my great surprise, it was as if heaven opened above us, and more than at any time in my life before, I experienced the love of God, a love so accepting and compassionate and that had eluded me for so many years. I had been a follower of Jesus for decades, but had lived all of my life with fear of God's wrath for sins and failures that I could never seem to escape or wipe clean.

In that moment with my father-in-law, and his reputation that had preceded him, I was brought into God's loving presence like never before, despite all of my efforts to keep my own reputation intact. In a few days, my father-in-law would become unresponsive and about two weeks later pass away into the arms of Jesus. But why had it taken one so obviously flawed, and who I thought so far from God, to lead me to God? I had begun praying with the assumption that I, the saint, was leading Kerry, the sinner to God. But it was the other way around. It was the so-called sinner leading the supposed saint, to God, in some ways for the very first time.

I used to think that Jesus hung out with sinners because they needed him so much, and this was true, of course. Still, the part I missed is that I wonder if Jesus wasn't also hoping that a few of those Pharisees and Jewish leaders working so hard to keep their own reputations intact might, as I did, also meet God for the very first time through the prayers of the broken and crooked people, whose reputations had long ago preceded them.

CHAPTER THIRTY-ONE

From Narrow Gate to a Multi-lane Highway to Zion
May 15, 2021

Growing up in Big Valley, PA, it was easy to imagine the truth of Jesus' words that "the gate is wide and the road easy that leads to destruction...For the gate is narrow, and the road is hard that leads to life, and there are few who find it." (Matthew 7:13-14) The roads in the valley were narrow, and not many people traveled them. The steep and narrow path up the Allison Gap to the outstanding view from the Big Rock was not for the faint of heart. The "flat road" was not easily accessible without four-wheel-drive vehicles. The walk during hunting season across the rocky and cold and windy "north side" of Hunting-don County was only negotiated by those genuinely dedicated to chas-ing deer around the mountain and calling it a "great day!"

Within a narrow valley where even Route 655, the "main road" that ran through the heart of the valley was narrow, yes, it was easy to imagine that we were indeed among the select few whom Jesus was talking about. Yes, we were the lucky ones. Lucky that we had found the narrow gate. Fortunate that we had found the narrow way that led to life. And lucky that we were not among those on that broad road leading to the destruction, an image reinforced by the revivalists who passed through the Valley.

Which I suspect was why I was so taken by the vision of Isaiah 40 that charismatic preacher Judson Cornwall described to me as I sat reading his little book *Freeway Under Construction* in the lower woods below our house as a young teenager. Judson said this:

> [The] turn of the century religious roads have no posted
> speed limits, but they are so narrow, crooked, and rough that
> no one can travel very fast and few travel very far. They were
> designed for the horse and buggy era [in Big Valley with its Old
> Order community, I could identify with that!] and have not
> been modernized. Little wonder, then, that few travelers are
> ever seen on the roads. An occasional sightseer or nostalgia buff
> may spend a Sunday on a slow drive, but the roads are mostly
> unused, except by those who have built residences along with
> them and use them for their personal estates.[14]

Wait a minute Judson! You seem to be suggesting that there was something wrong with the narrow roads and paths that I grew up with that were traveled only by the lucky ones, the special ones, the saved ones, those who happened to be born on those paths. But Judson, what about Jesus' words of that narrow gate and narrow road for the lucky ones and that wide gate and broad path for our damned neighbors?

But Judson continued:

> Still, men have an inner yearning after God. The cry for
> righteousness that has been heralded in our nation in the past
> few years is but an indication of an embryonic craving for the
> God of righteousness...a deep hunger for God himself. When
> the hunger grips the world, as the prophets have declared it
> would, there must be a rapid, safe, enjoyable route of access to
> God. The rituals, catechisms, religious activities, and trappings

---

14   Judson Cornwall, *Freeway Under Construction By Order of Isaiah 40:3-5* (NJ: Logos, 1978), 3-4.

will not appeal to this group of people. They will need a multi-lane freeway into God's presence, and the time to build it is before it is desperately needed.[15]

The idea that "there must be a rapid, safe" and especially an "enjoyable route" to God must have both challenged but also rung with hope in my teenage heart so tormented by my strenuous efforts to stay on the narrow path but continuously finding myself so unable to do so. What was so wrong with me that I, among the lucky ones, couldn't seem to stay between the lines and didn't find staying between the lines very enjoyable either?

But here was a theology so different, so attractive, so expansive, so inviting. Was Judson a heretic? I'm sure that I hoped not, for his words indeed sounded like good news. Judson believed that the ultimate vision of God was for all flesh to see "the glory of the Lord," but only after the "way of the Lord" has been excavated and mountains removed and valleys raised to make this grand highway to Zion. And the invitation that Judson held out to this tormented teenager was that there was room in this grand excavation project for even me. And perhaps the road wasn't as hard to stay on as I imagined!

Judson's view is that the death and resurrection of Christ and then the coming of the Spirit changed everything, that Jesus was now the Way by which God had orchestrated a plan that would provide an opportunity for all humankind to know God. And indeed this is the vision of the "last days" of the ancient prophets in which "the earth will be filled with the knowledge of the glory of the Lord as the waters cover the sea" (Habakkuk 2:14) and Jeremiah 31:34, where "No longer will they teach their neighbor, or say to one another 'Know the Lord,' because they will all know me, from the least of them to the greatest," declares the Lord.

---

[15]   Freeway, 4.

So was Jesus wrong about the narrow way and the few who find it? Of course not! But I wonder to what extent his words were descriptive of what so often is the case, but that does not represent the fullness of God's heart, a heart that "so loved the world" and that "desires that none shall perish."

The problem with imagining that we are lucky to have found the narrow gate and the difficult path to Zion is that we too often become self-righteous, hypocritical, and exclusive. Like the Pharisees, we too often "pile heavy burdens on people's shoulders and won't lift a finger to help." Like them, "we lock people out of the kingdom of heaven," and like them, we "travel over land and sea to win one follower" only to "make that person twice as fit for hell as [we] are." (Luke 11:3,13,15 NRSV)

Sometimes the people of the narrow road and narrow gate assume that as the special, the chosen, the lucky, and the few, we are also called to be the gatekeepers to the broad highway that the Spirit is building to Glory—preventing ourselves and others from joining the Spirit's inclusive project? What if we instead got on with the lowering of those mountains and raising of those valleys and making the crooked places straight and rough places smooth so that our neighbors, co-workers, friends, enemies, and families might have an easier time discovering the Light of Life, of finding their way Home.

But we can't engage in the dismantling work of Isaiah 40 until we've been dismantled ourselves, until we've been stripped of any sense that we are the lucky ones, until we understand just how broken and crooked we are ourselves, and until our hearts break for the brokenness in the world as if we were crying in pain for our own brokenness.

A listener asked me this week if I was suggesting that they shut the doors of their church and just give up—was that what I was saying? I replied that every fellowship of Jesus' followers must discern for themselves what the Spirit is saying. But I'm not sure how much of the decision is even in our hands, for the Spirit seems to be hard at work closing quite a few churches that have become narrow roads of the lucky ones rather than saints who in their love for a world that God so loved are hard at work on that multi-lane freeway that runs right into the heart of God!

CHAPTER THIRTY-TWO

Will You Have Coffee With Me?
December 21, 2020

For whatever reason, as much as I have enjoyed writing and recording these Advent podcasts this season, I have found myself feeling quite dry spiritually, or perhaps it's the sense that I should be feeling more deeply the reality of the Christ-child's coming. I had prepared a message to share with our congregation that focused exclusively on that Child's coming, and then suddenly swerved early Sunday morning and changed directions entirely, bringing a message that reflected on the events of this past year. I encouraged the congregation to do so within the context of the coming Kingdom and the new heaven and new earth.

Did I swerve at the last minute because the Spirit led me, or did I bend because I'm unsure what to do with the Savior this year? Earlier in Advent, I preached messages of the shepherds and the wise men, but why in the world couldn't I get an inspiring sermon together about the One who brought the Good News that I say I believe? I don't have a clear answer—did I hear God's Spirit or listen to myself? I'm not sure.

But I know that I awoke this morning with the book of Revelation, chapter 3, on my mind. The book of Revelation begins with Jesus, having returned to the Father, now bringing words of correction and encouragement to seven little churches established as the result of the apostles' missionary efforts. The harshest words of Jesus are reserved for the last church, Laodicea, a wealthy church, a con-

135

fident church, but a church that Christ threatens to spit out of his mouth.

I grew up always imagining that I was a member of Laodicea and that I resided just on the tip of Jesus's tongue, waiting at any moment for Jesus to do just what he said—spew me out into, I imagined, eternal death. I lived on the edge of terror—envisioning lukewarmness all around and within me.

At the same time, I grew up with that painting of Jesus, that many of us have seen, where Christ stands outside of a door, waiting for that door to be opened by whoever is on the inside. It was an inviting painting of a Jesus who patiently waits for us to get off the couch, to wake up, to lay down the remote, to close the refrigerator door, or to give up and stop doing whatever might be keeping us from responding to his gentle knock.

A few years ago, I suddenly recognized that the painting of this kind and patient and waiting Jesus at the door was from the same passage in Revelation 3 that included the threatening "I will spew you out of my mouth" Jesus. How could this be? Why hadn't someone helped me see that though Jesus cautions that he will correct us, he is also the same One who has infinite love that awaits the opening of the door of our hearts if only a crack? And that any threat of "spewing" emerges from the love of One so significant that he can hardly handle hearing us weeping behind that closed door, crying because we feel so alone, weeping because we've been damaged and tossed away, weeping because trauma has left us without hope, weeping because we've lost the very person who we most loved in the world, crying because we've been misunderstood, because we know we are lukewarm but have no idea how to warm up, weeping because it is all we know how to do anymore.

After Heidi and I reunited following a lengthy separation early in our marriage, we incorporated a little ritual into our relationship—we have coffee together. It's not the caffeine of course, that matters so much—though admittedly some days it helps—but rather the habit or ritual of coming together to repair after a conflict or to have a difficult conversation or to resolve whatever was in the way of our hearing each other just an hour before.

We sometimes now say that coffee has saved our marriage! If, following a difficult moment, one of us says, "Would you like coffee?" and the other says "yes," then we both know the repair of our relationship is on its way. But if one says "no" to the coffee invitation, we know there is still time needed or work to be done before we can get to that table together again.

You see, friend, this is all that Jesus wants—no matter who you are, what you've done, where you've been, whatever the sins committed or omitted—he just wants to have coffee with you. He only wants to be with you. Is there work to be done in my life and heart? A ton of it, for sure. But before Jesus and I get around to renovating my heart, he first wants to take a coffee break and hear what's going on inside my heart. For it just might be that in doing so, I also listen for the first time to what is going on within me.

I tell my students that I've come to understand that they will never learn if they live in shame. The same is true for us—we will never change if shame is the motivation. And God knew that too— that's one reason he came as a baby to us and not as a King or Warrior or Jewish Nationalist. He came not with a crown on his head or a sword by his side but with a coffee cup in his hand. Jesus' first interest is in knowing us, hearing us, and letting us know we are loved. For he recognizes that we will never trust him to change us if we don't trust him to love us, and well, crack the door to hear him ask, "Can we have coffee together?"

CHAPTER THIRTY-THREE

A Messed-up Kid and That Pentecostal Preacher With Good News
May 1, 2021

In my somewhat chaotic stacks of books, I recently found that little gem I had been looking for by Judson Cornwall, a book by a Pentecostal preacher that first introduced my imagination to that grand excavation project of Isaiah 40 where mountains would be lowered, valleys raised, rough places made a plain, and crooked places straight. As a kid, this book had captured my attention as I read and reread its 58 pages down in the woods below our home. For it was there, among the birds, squirrels, and flowing stream that my mind found solace from the continual condemnation and shame, and it was there that my heart was awakened to the truth that both the church I knew and the person I was, had a lot of dismantling ahead of us. At the time, I didn't see the work that such dismantling would incur, nor the pain, nor the resistance.

But this little book that cost me just 95 cents, would give me a vision and hope to confront the damnation I so often felt. And perhaps it was this vision so imaginatively articulated by charismatic preacher Judson Cornwall that helped to keep me with Jesus for the many years of mental and spiritual struggle that still lay ahead for me.

Cornwall's little book entitled *Freeway Under Construction by Order of Isaiah 40:3-5*, as I reread it several times this past week, articulates nearly everything I've been saying over this year and validates my prayer that God would dismantle the church and dismantle my life however he needs to do that.

I recently heard a preacher pray something that I hear so often: "God, please build up the church, so the gates of hell will not prevail against it." When I hear such prayers I never know what a built-up church looks like exactly, though I suspect what most of us have in mind is some current version of the church-industrial complex that the Spirit is trying to bring to its knees in this very moment. But what I know is that it was the dismantling of our Lord on a cross that would break the power of the gates of hell. So it is hard for me to imagine it won't also be a dismantled church and dismantled preachers and dismantled saints and sinners of all sorts that also once again overcome the enemy of our souls. For it is only the dismantled ones who know they can't do so alone.

The message of dismantledness is most often received by those who know themselves to be already broken, by those who I call the diaspora of the church who are on the run from the church if not from God, by those wounded and traumatized by the church, by those who've given up on the church, by those who have learned they have no place in the church. Little do these folks know that they are often closer to sainthood and the Kingdom than those within the church who resist the message of dismantling of both self and religious structures and ideology.

In a chapter entitled "The Bulldozers Are Coming," Judson Cornwall describes the dismantling that the Spirit wants to do in each of our lives, and that God must be able to do if we are going to be useful for the grand excavation project that will lead to the glory of God as promised in Isaiah 40. Cornwall says this:

> What tears we shed at this stage of construction in our
> lives. Everywhere we look, we see devastation and ruin. The
> Spirit has successfully removed everything but has replaced

nothing. We are not only naked but exposed to all lookers. In a small way, we find ourselves sharing in the ravishment and shame of Christ's cross...and after the Spirit begins to work in our lives, we don't look very much like a victorious, over-coming, empowered Christian either. We are so marred and deformed that we merely look like a mess. But remember, we're his mess! He did it to us. Oh, he probably used the help of loved ones, fellow believers, the unconverted, and perhaps even the devil, but it was all at his command. He did it![16]

Friends, do you see why this message brought such comfort to a kid tormented by the chronic belief that I was never good enough, a message promoted in those Brunk tent revivals and by a religious culture that for centuries believed that "mantling" the mess was the way to heaven even if it made being a Christian hell on this side of eternity? The vision articulated by Judson Cornwall dismantled that message and told me that, of course, I was a mess, that I was God's mess, and that the only way to be used in the Spirit's grand excavation project was to admit that I was indeed a mess.

And I'm still a mess. But I'm God's mess. And I've learned that the saints over time, if indeed they are saints at all, universally acknowledge that they are messes too. Just look at the language of St. Paul to describe himself the older he got! "The worst of sinners" he called himself.

---

[16]   Freeway, 21.

CHAPTER THIRTY-FOUR

I Wish They Had Told Me That I Was Dead!

September 20, 2021

Heidi and I returned this weekend from a time of rest and renewal and beautiful moments of connection with each other as well as with our children and grandson, delighted as he is by the ocean and sand and full of wonder at the newness he encounters daily. It is clear why God gives us grandchildren in the sunset of our lives, for as I've learned, all things look different in the sunset than in the sunrise. More beauty, more gratitude, more reflection, appreciation, kindness, understanding, and expectation.

As I left the beach for that last evening, with sadness that another year in our favorite spot had come to an end, I also remembered that someday there will be no end to a moment such as this one, where sunrise and sunset will come together in a place of rest and peace and glory that multiplies many times over the most extraordinary beauty we've ever experienced on this side of the sunset that lies ahead.

While on vacation I read the story of Reynolds Price, author, and poet who was diagnosed with a debilitating spinal tumor at 51 years of age.[17] Professor of English at Duke University, Price found himself facing an end-of-life sunset. The best medical experts said

---

[17]   Reynolds Price, *A Whole New Life: An Illness and a Healing* (New York: Scribner Books, 2003).

they could extend his days six months at the most. Instead, he lived more than two more decades—in chronic pain and a wheelchair.

Price's story is the first one, in all of the stories I have read and heard over the past five years since I began to tremor, with which I most identify, other than that story in John 9 of the blind man whom Jesus healed and who for his healing, was kicked out of the temple. For it is not only prophets who are rejected in their home-towns; it can also happen to those who believe in that Prophet and who are converted by the love of that Prophet. Ironic, isn't it?

"But we know Jesus," we all say. "But we've been born again," we hear. "But we've been converted—it happened as a child," we utter. And therein lies the rub—it happened as a child or, for that matter, "it happened six years ago or six weeks ago." But unless it happens every day, conversion just might mean very little.

Reynolds Price, looking back four years at his original diag-nosis, wished in retrospect that when he awoke from his lengthy surgery, someone would have had the courage to tell him that he had died—that the Reynolds he and others knew was now dead, gone, had kicked the bucket forever. For he would never be the same. His death sentence, his suffering, his awareness of the sunset ahead—this and more would forever transform him, forever lead him into a life and down a path he had never been before.

Suffering and breakage and death can do that to those who are open to the fantastic possibilities that lie ahead, for the seed that allows itself to accept its buriedness, and to believe beyond belief that within death lies a door that had up to that point remained unopened. The problem is that most of us will turn from that door, and though the way back to who we were is now closed, we will kick and scream and claw as if it were not, and as we do so, we will day-dream of what was and is now gone. But somehow, the daydreams eventually become nightmares, and who we could have become had we chosen that door is lost in the memory of what was, but now can never be.

This is what I have tried over the past year to say to the church—that we are dead. There is no going back. God in his mercy is dismantling us. There is a new door to open—where a glorious future lies ahead. The purpose of all our dismantlings is so that Jesus would be revealed, and in the process, that we might be converted by the love of Jesus all over again. And in fact, Jesus does show up to Reynolds Price, a pagan and heathen in the eyes of many of us who can recount the day we were first converted but haven't been converted since.

The Dedication to the first book in this series entitled *A Church Dismantled—A Kingdom Restored: Why is God Taking Apart the Church?* is dedicated to my dear wife and companion, Heidi: "God knew that I needed a partner who would already be there waiting for me when I finally showed up as my most authentic self."

But without this experience of Parkinson's disease that has brought death to who I was, and without Heidi willing to accept not only who I am but who I am becoming, my authentic self would never have shown its face. And it is hard to tell how I would have ever made my way Home. And until the church can assume that this dismantling is of God's Spirit, it will fail to become its resurrected self, bursting forth into that new day where sunset and sunrise merge into the One. And if it cannot, Home may just remain beyond its grasp.

But thankfully, with God, all things are possible.